W9-BRA-719

2495

12/9/4

ROBOTICS

FACTS ON FILE
SCIENCE SOURCEBOOKS

ROBOTICS

THE MARRIAGE OF COMPUTERS AND MACHINES

ELLEN THRO

Facts On File®

AN INFOBASE HOLDINGS COMPANY

ROBOTICS: THE MARRIAGE OF COMPUTERS AND MACHINES

Copyright © 1993 by Ellen Thro

Facts On File, Inc.
460 Park Avenue South
New York NY 10016

Library of Congress Cataloging-in-Publication Data
Thro, Ellen.
   Robotics : the marriage of computers and machines / Ellen Thro.
     p. cm. — (Facts On File science sourcebooks)
   Includes bibliographical references and index.
   Summary: Introduces the science of robotics, discussing the nature of artificial intelligence, the history of robotics, the different kinds of robots, and their uses.
   ISBN 0-8160-2628-9
   1. Robotics—History—Juvenile literature. [1. Robotics.
2. Robots.] I. Title. II. Series.
TJ211.2.T47 1993
629.8'92—dc20   92-16308

A British CIP catalogue record for this book is available from the British Library.

Facts On File books are available at special discounts when purchased in bulk quantities for businesses, associations, institutions or sales promotions. Please contact our Special Sales Department in New York at 212/683-2244 or 800/322-8755.

Text design by Ron Monteleone
Jacket design by Amy Gonzalez
On the cover: An industrial robot (photo courtesy of FPG International,
  © T. Tracy, 1991)
Composition by Facts On File, Inc.
Manufactured by the Maple-Vail Book Manufacturing Group
Printed in the United States of America

10 9 8 7 6 5 4 3 2

This book is printed on acid-free paper.

CONTENTS

ACKNOWLEDGMENTS

Numerous people have helped make this book a reality. Special appreciation goes to Barbara Lucas of Lucas-Evans Books, Commander Bart Everett of the Naval Oceans Systems Center, Pat Kelly at the Balboa Naval Hospital, and to Nicole Bowen, the editor of this book series, and her staff. My thanks to all.

1 THE ROBOT FAMILY TREE

What is a robot? An explorer of the ocean floor? A pioneer in outer space? A fast-food cook? A coal miner? An auto worker? A surgeon's assistant?

A robot can be all of these—and more. Of course a robot is a machine, but a very special one. It is also an independent being. For centuries the idea of the robot has included our powers to think, create, and control—the skills we believe make us unique among the creatures of the Earth.

The modern definition of a robot classifies it as a machine with these parts:

- a *program* that tells it what to do
- an arm, hand, or other moving part that performs a useful *action*, like lifting, assembling, or moving something
- one or more *sensors*, so it can tell the difference between what it's working on and everything else
- a *decision maker* to decide whether to perform the action
- a *controller*, which is in charge of overall operations

Today's robots are at work in factories and hazardous environments throughout the industrialized world. Research going on right now will produce robots with even greater skills and even intelligence.

The first modern robots were built in the 1950s, but the robot family tree goes back thousands of years. The oldest of its three branches begins with dancing dolls, or marionettes, in ancient Egypt and talking statues in ancient Greece. The other two branches are much younger—factory machines and computers.

These nonrobotic, but real, ancestors are just part of the family tree. Robots have fictional ancestors, too: *androids*, robots that are practically human, and *cyborgs*, beings that are part human and part robot.

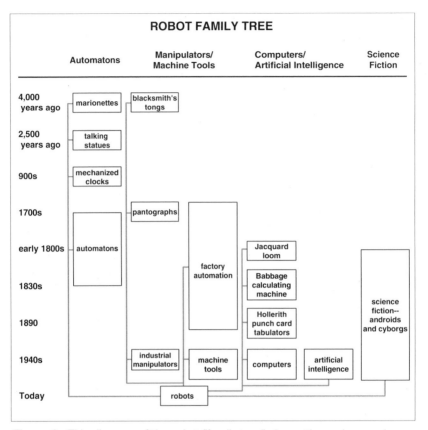

Figure 1: This diagram of the robot "family tree" shows the various real and fictional branches that came together in the 20th century with the creation of robots.

So far androids and cyborgs live only on TV and movie screens and on book pages. They express the hopes and possibilities for real robots. They also present the fears people have about robots. And they make all of us ask a basic question: What does it mean to be human?

The First Robots

Robot is a 20th-century word, and modern computer-driven robots are products of this century. But people have been building self-operating systems for centuries. They are called *automatons*, powered by air, water, or mechanics. Thousands of years before automatons there were dolls and statues that acted like humans.

Dancing Dolls and Speaking Statues

Marionettes are puppets with strings attached to their joints, so that a person can make them move. They're used as actors in plays put on in miniature theaters. The people who pull the strings are concealed behind the scenes. To an audience, the dolls behave like people. Strange as it may seem, marionettes are related to robots.

The oldest branch of the robot family tree reaches back 4,000 years to Egypt, at the time the pyramids were built. Marionettes designed to sing, clap, and dance have been found in Egyptian burial pyramids. Archaeologists tell us that some of the dancing dolls were used in religious burial services. Some dolls represented the survivors, acting for them by sending food along on the death journey. Still others symbolized the transfer of money and power from the dead person to the survivors.

In ancient Greece, statues that "talked" were used to "bring" messages from the next world. Hidden priests and priestesses did the actual talking. People believed that by talking, the statues represented life, or even that they really were alive.

Automatons

Automatons, or self-operating systems, were first made and used about a thousand years ago in the Middle East and Europe. Mechanical clocks were popular throughout the Islamic world from the 9th to the 14th centuries. By the 15th century, Europe was filled with elaborate church clocks featuring people moving arms, lifting hammers, and striking bells, and even whole moving religious processions. The clock in St. Mark's Cathedral in Venice, Italy, is one famous example.

By the 16th century, smaller mechanical clocks ticked, chimed, and moved on walls and tables throughout the royal courts of Europe, the Near East, and Asia. But keeping track of time was just the beginning. There were mechanical drink dispensers, rolling down the banquet table and stopping at each place. And there were mechanical garden fountains. There was an automated wash basin that filled with water when someone came near, then extended a hand holding a piece of pumice stone (instead of soap). When the person picked up the stone, the automaton drew back its hand. And there were mechanical puppet theaters, complete with singing birds, hissing dragons, and moving people.

Alive and Not Alive

What is it about the human body that makes it alive, while a lawn mower or a car isn't? The ancient Greeks thought it was the ability to speak. Today scientists consider being alive to mean the ability to transfer genes from one generation to another. People inherit genes from their parents and pass them on to their children. The same is true for cats, trees, and even bacteria.

But there was a time when scientists pondered the idea that people might be alive because they are able to move around. That thought made sense in the 17th century, when modern science began. Isaac Newton became famous by formulating the laws of motion. In fact, motion seemed to be so important that scientists decided it was the guiding principle of the universe. It was just a short jump to the idea that motion was also what made people alive.

In the 17th century interest in automatons increased and changed. The word *automaton* was coined then. People began asking, can we design and build machines to move so naturally that they are actually alive? A scientist in those days who wanted to build what the 17th-century philosopher Thomas Hobbes called an "artificial mann" that moved might have asked several questions about it. Would it be alive? Could it think? Have emotions? Tell right from wrong? Be creative?

By the early 18th-century, inventors were trying to answer these questions by building automatons that were amazingly lifelike. They were based on another branch of the new science—anatomy. If we make the automaton anatomically correct, they thought, there was a good chance that it will be "alive." Philosophers, alchemists, magicians, priests, and even kings all took part in automaton-building.

Two of the most lifelike of these automatons were a flute player and a duck, both the creations of an 18th-century French inventor, Jacques de Vaucanson. His flute player was a man-sized figure of a faun—a mythical creature half-man–half- goat—seated on a rock and playing a flute. The most amazing thing wasn't the way the flute player looked, but what it did. It could hold any flute. It could take air into its lungs, blow into the flute with several different lip movements and tongue placements, and cover the flute's holes with its fingers to play a tune. The whole thing was controlled by a turning cylinder covered with raised bars, like those used in music boxes. The bars in turn pushed levers, rods, and chains to produce the flute player's movements.

Vaucanson was experimenting with more than the body of his automaton. According to a common 18th-century belief, by giving his creation the ability to make music, he was also giving it a human voice—the voice of emotion.

Vaucanson also built an automated duck that quacked, drank, went into the water, lifted its feathers, spread its tail, and flapped its wings.

[Engraving by Gravelot, from *Jacques Vaucanson Mecanicien de Génie* by André Doyon and Lucien Liaigre]

This 1738 engraving shows three autom-atons made by Jacques de Vaucanson; the duck is in the center and the flute player on the right.

It even had a ducklike digestive tract. The duck could take grain from Vaucanson's hand, swallow it, digest the grain (dissolved in water) in its stomach, and excrete it through an anus with a sphincter muscle. The inventor even left the digestive system partly exposed so people could see how it worked.

Vaucanson's creations greatly impressed the French king Louis XV. At one point, Vaucanson planned a working model of the human circulatory system. Louis offered to send him to South America, so he could experiment with a new discovery, called rubber, for the model's veins and arteries.

Later Automatons

Many automatons that mimicked living systems were built during the 18th and early 19th centuries. Their main purpose was to entertain the public and, of course, to make money. Wind-up automatons played the organ, wrote letters with pen and ink, and drew figures with a pencil. One, called the "Great Magician," even performed mind-reading tricks. A French father-and-son team named Jaquet-Droz built various automatons that played instruments, "wrote," and "drew," all controlled by music-box disks.

Sophisticated Parisians loved the lifelike machines. But not everybody was impressed. The historian Linda Strauss has found an 18th-century tale about a village woman who mistakes an automaton for a very talented person. When the woman discovers its true identity, she immediately decides it isn't so talented after all. Anything that an automaton can do isn't much of a human talent!

Probably the most famous—and mysterious—automaton was a chess-playing machine called The Turk, created in Vienna, Austria, in 1769 by the Baron von Kempelen. Kempelen exhibited a chessboard-topped box, presided over by the life-sized figure of a man dressed in a turban and gown. Controlled by levers and pulleys, The Turk played chess against human opponents and usually won. Kempelen always began his demonstration by opening the cabinet, to show that no one was hidden inside. But questions were raised for decades. Was it really a smart automaton? Or was The Turk's expert-

(from U.S. Atomic Energy Commission, Office of Information Services)

The Turk, a chess-playing automaton, was created in 1769 by Baron von Kempelen.

level game really controlled by a chess-playing child, midget, or amputee? Or by a series of them over the years?

Kempelen exhibited his machine throughout Europe until his death in 1804. A new owner then continued the tours into the 1840s.

Many people tried to explain the machine's success or expose it as a hoax. One debunker was the 19th-century American writer Edgar Allan Poe. The question was never answered to everyone's satisfaction.

Interestingly, chess has always been considered a true test of computer programming skill. So The Turk was a forerunner of modern, "intelligent," computer chess-playing programs.

By the end of the 19th century, automatons had mostly disappeared. Even so, a few were built as late as 1939. At the same time, the other two branches of the robot family were growing and expanding—computers and factory machines.

Computers

At the same time that The Turk was mystifying people in the early 19th century, the modern computer had its beginnings. The location wasn't a scientist's laboratory but a silk factory in Lyon, France. A weaver named Joseph-Marie Jacquard invented a punched card system for weaving elaborate designs. The card holes controlled which warp threads were raised for the shuttle (weft) to pass under. This in turn determined the finished color and pattern of the fabric. Jacquard's system revolutionized the weaving industry. It is still used today around the world.

A few decades later Charles Babbage, an English mathematician, was influenced by Jacquard's loom cards. He invented a series of mechanical calculating machines. Babbage and his assistant, Ada, countess of Lovelace, laid the foundation for modern computer science.

Punched cards went electric in the late 1800s. The American Herman Hollerith invented a punched card tabulating machine for use in the 1890 United States Census. Information from census interviews was punched into the cards. Then it was tabulated as the cards were run through the system. Each hole permitted an electrical signal to be produced and counted. Hollerith's company merged with the firm that eventually became the computer giant IBM. Updated punch card systems are in use today as, for example, voting machines.

The first computers were built in the United States and Britain in the 1940s. They were huge, building-sized machines that used bulky vacuum tubes to produce and change electrical signals. The transistor, invented in 1947 by the Americans John Bardeen, Walter Brattain, and William Shockley, showed that small pieces of silicon could do the same thing. Teams of transistors called integrated circuits—computer chips—led to today's powerful computers in tiny packages.

Factory Automation

Automation—the technique of making a process automatic—is a word that means different things to different generations. The word was coined in the late 1940s to describe machines doing the same factory work that people were doing. But the idea has been around since the Industrial Revolution (18th and 19th centuries). Huge water- or steam-powered factory machines replaced hand labor. The jacquard loom was an example. Yet those machines required large numbers of workers to tend them.

A century ago, the automobile automated the horsedrawn carriage. But the driver had to provide physical force to crank (start) the engine, shift gears, apply the brakes, and steer the vehicle. Forty years ago, power steering, power brakes, and automatic transmission automated cars further.

Self-defrosting refrigerators automated the process of hand-chipping the ice that built up inside. The old refrigerator, in turn, had automated the box that required hand-loading of a block of ice every day.

There have also been several generations of factory automation. The assembly line, popularized by Henry Ford in the 1910s, was a big step forward. Building a car had been a complex process. It required skilled workers who could make decisions. The assembly line made factories more efficient by breaking the process into a series of simple tasks. The workers needed only limited skills and didn't make decisions, so they could be paid much lower wages.

This change led to charges that workers were being turned into "machines." Labor union demands and protective laws improved both working conditions and wages in many places.

At the same time, this system led to the next step in factory automation. Machines alone could do some of the simple tasks, replacing workers entirely. These machines came to be called *machine tools*.

Machine Tools

In the United States today, anything made from two or more pieces of metal, wood, plastic, or other materials was probably produced with machine tools. These machines cut, drill, and grind. They turn out many identical copies of the same item. The hole is always drilled or the pieces welded in the same place, just as if a person carefully did the work by hand.

The most accurate machine tools are computerized, with *numerical control*. This system uses numbers to describe the shape of the part and the tool's movements and working speed. There are even computer languages just for numerical control machine tools. But they're still just tools. They don't work the way people do. Industrial robots were the next step.

Industrial Robots

Some people may question whether industrial robots are just fancier machine tools? Or are there real differences? There are differences, even if they're not always clear. In fact, the same machine can be called a robot in one country and a machine tool in another. But in general, robots are more flexible. They're more precise and accurate. And they make decisions.

Industrial robots generally have guidance systems that put them at just the right place in front of their working materials. Their sensory systems tell them whether conditions are right to perform the task. Most robots are programmed to take the next step, deciding whether to go ahead with the task.

Factory automation today depends on two things—decision making and flexibility. A modern factory doesn't make just one product all the time. It must quickly change from one model to another, or even from one product to another. Robots let many manufacturers compete in the world marketplace.

Today's robots are still the first generation, the first products of all four branches of the robot family tree. In factories they work as welders and painters. They assemble products and perform pick-and-place jobs (picking up materials and placing the finished product somewhere else).

Outside of the factory, robots must be flexible enough to move around on varied landscapes for firefighting and other hazardous or changing situations. Tomorrow's robots will be more independent, intelligent, and perhaps more human.

The people who have built automatons and robots have wondered what being alive meant. They've asked, what's the difference between the movement of machines and the movement of people and other living things? What they thought usually depended on three things: the technology of the day, their knowledge of how the human body works, and their beliefs (philosophy and religion).

These same ideas are expressed by fictional robots, the ones in TV shows, movies, and books.

Fictional Robots

- When does a robot behave so much like a person that it too is human?
- Do robots know what they are?
- What human qualities do they have? Can they acquire those qualities? Or get rid of them?

These questions apply to a favorite robot of the 1990s, *Star Trek*'s Commander Data, who wants humor. They also apply to favorite robots of the early 1900s, like the Land of Oz's Tin Woodman, who wanted a heart.

Early Fictional Robots

The oldest robot-related story is probably the Greek myth of Pygmalion, a king who fell in love with a statue he made. Pygmalion prayed to Aphrodite, the goddess of love, who made the statue come alive.

Two stories involve beings handmade of natural materials. In 16th-century European Jewish legend, the Golem was an automaton made of earth by a man who gave it life using a combination of faith and magic. In 1818 Mary Godwin Shelley wrote the novel *Frankenstein*, about a scientist of that name who created a creature out of body parts. Frankenstein then brought it to life. The creature was intelligent and sensitive. But it was also hideously ugly, so it was rejected by people. In revenge, it turned killer.

The Golem and Frankenstein's monster tell us about ourselves, as well as about robots. For this reason they live on into our time. Both have been made into movies and borrowed by modern authors.

The 19th-century American author Edgar Allan Poe is called the father of the modern mystery story. But he was also an early science fiction writer. His story "The Man That Was Used Up," written in 1839, describes a human whose damaged arms and legs were replaced by mechanical substitutes. The character was a forerunner of the cyborg, and his mechanical limbs were forerunners of the "intelligent" artificial limbs now being developed for handicapped people.

A late-19th-century story by another American, Ambrose Bierce, was influenced by Poe's analysis of The Turk. "Moxon's Master" features an android that strangles its maker, who has defeated it in a chess game.

L. Frank Baum began writing the Oz series of books almost a century ago. The books are filled with automatons, androids, and cyborgs. The most famous are the Tin Woodman and the Scarecrow, who also appear in the movie version of *The Wonderful Wizard of Oz*. The Tin Woodman is really a cyborg that began as a human. He replaced his human body parts one by one with parts of tin, following a series of witch-induced accidents with his ax. The Scarecrow came to life as it was being constructed.

Other "live" Oz automatons with human qualities are Scraps, the patchwork doll; the Sawhorse; and the Gump, a flying sofa. The Glass Cat had the human quality of compassion because it had a heart. Tik-tok, the mechanical man, was intelligent because it had brains (made of stainless steel). It spoke, thought, and acted logically, at least when it was wound up. But it wasn't alive. Tik-tok was proud of that fact even if this did let the "live" automatons feel superior.

The word *robot* appeared in 1921, coined by Czechoslovakian writer Karel Capek for his play, *R.U.R.* (which stands for Rossum's Universal Robots). *Robot* is taken from the Czech word for forced labor. In the play, Rossum's Universal Robots look like people and have the human ability to kill. But they lack two things: a history and the imperfections that go along with being human. Eventually they kill off the entire human race. However, a chemical exists to give the robots emotions. At the end of the play, a male and a female robot have become human themselves, the founders of a new, intelligent race.

Only a few years after *R.U.R.* the first movie about robots came along. It was *Metropolis*, a 1926 silent film by the German director Fritz Lang, and today considered a film classic. The story tells of a future when factory workers have become little more than machines in the production system. The workers try to rebel, but a robot built by the evil factory owners leads them to their destruction.

A futuristic dance partner? Elektro entertained visitors at the 1940 New York World's Fair. He could walk, move his head, arms and fingers, count on his fingers, distinguish colors, and smoke. He could also speak 77 words. Weighing 260 pounds and standing seven feet tall, Elektro was the latest of several mechanical men Westinghouse built, starting in 1927.

[Courtesy of Westinghouse Historical Collection]

Primitive Early Robots

At the time that fiction and movies about robots were gaining popularity, science was moving ahead. In 1927 engineers at Westinghouse Electric and Manufacturing Company began working on a series of mechanical men. The first, called Televox, was created that year. In 1932 Willie Vocalite was "born." He toured the United States, entertaining and astounding people just as the earlier automatons had done. After Televox came Elektro, who appeared at the 1940 New York World's Fair with his dog Sparko. Both were the creation of Joseph Melton Barnett, a Westinghouse engineer.

When Barnett spoke, Elektro obeyed. The spoken words caused vibrations that were converted into electrical waves, which then raised a shutter in front of a lamp and sent a flash of light to the photoelectric tube, or "electric eye," that served as Elektro's brain. This light was then converted back into an electric current, which started Elektro's motors. In this way Elektro walked, spoke, and

(Courtesy of Westinghouse Historical Collection)

Elektro is shown here with Sparko, his "canine" companion, and their creator Joseph Barnett. Sparko was a 65-pound Scotty made of aluminum, steel, motors, gears, and switches. Standing a little over a foot tall and measuring 29 inches long, he ran behind Elektro, sat, stood up, wagged his tail, cocked his head, barked, whined, and growled.

performed in other ways, making robots seem like a reality to those who saw him.

The 1940s and 1950s

During the 1940s and 1950s, three developments made modern robotics a reality: computers, artificial intelligence, and the study of systems.

At about the same time that computer development began in the early 1940s, the British mathematician Alan Turing and other computer developers began to ask the question, can computers actually think for themselves? It was the beginning of artificial intelligence studies.

Also in the 1940s, the American mathematician Norbert Wiener and other scientists began studying systems. They studied how the human body's vision, motion, brain, and other systems resembled machine systems that did the same work. This was the field called *cybernetics*. It grew into several modern fields, including cognitive science (the study of human and computer thought).

Robots—not automatons or "mechanical men"—controlled by brainlike computers and possessing some sort of intelligence, now seemed possible. In actuality, it would take at least several decades before any sort of "intelligent" robot was developed. In the meantime, fiction hurried to catch up with theory.

Modern Fictional Robots

The science fiction stories of Isaac Asimov in the 1940s and 1950s, such as *I, Robot*, explored the benefits of robots in a future society. Asimov wrote what he called the Three Laws of Robotics. According to the laws, robots are allowed to protect themselves, but only if they don't disobey or harm humans. Many computer scientists began using these fictional laws as they developed real robots.

Other writers have used this background to explore what it means to be human in a robotic world. For example, the hero of Anne McCaffrey's 1969 book *The Ship Who Sang* is Helva, a physically deformed baby who could never live on her own. Helva was given freedom, mobility, and the chance to express her intellect and emotions by being permanently grafted into a spaceship.

Movies also examined the effects of humans and robots on each other. Like people, some film robots were evil and some were good. For the first time, some robots were even lovable.

The first robot to capture the public's affection was Robbie, in the 1950s film *Forbidden Planet*, a science fiction version of Shakespeare's play *The Tempest*. The good-natured Robbie was handy around the human outpost on an alien world, as well as being a protector and skilled worker. He was followed on the screen by the three plant-tending robots Huey, Dewey, and Louie (named for Donald Duck's nephews) in the 1972 *Silent Running*.

Probably the most famous of the lovable and intelligent robots were the *Star Wars* films' R2D2 and C3PO, from the late 1970s and early 1980s. The 1980s also gave us Number Five, an advanced sentry robot brought to life by an electrical accident in *Short Circuit*—a favorite of real-life robot scientists.

The Robbie-like robot on *Lost in Space* and the human cyborgs on *The Six Million Dollar Man* and *The Bionic Woman*, accompanied by Max, the bionic dog, brought the same admirable qualities to TV. (Hymie, the bumbling but earnest robot on the 1960s comedy series *Get Smart*, was played strictly for laughs—and satire.) The 1990s so far have given us Commander Data, the android Star Fleet officer on *Star Trek: The Next Generation*, who constantly tries to understand what it means to be human and to develop human qualities himself.

All this goodness has been balanced through the years by evil robots and cyborgs. TV has given us the Darth Vader–like Cylons on *Battlestar Galactica* and the Daleks in the British *Dr. Who* series. The lethal gunfighter robot of the 1973 film *Westworld* was a commentary on modern recreation, and on movies about the Old West. The robot was played by Yul Brynner, who had played gunfighters in several westerns. More recently, Arnold Schwarzenegger's ruthless cyborgs have been box office hits.

Conclusion

The human desire to use the power of our knowledge and imagination to create lifelike beings has given us automatons and fictional robots. So far, we lack the ability to make real living robots. We cannot yet make beings with genes to be inherited, let alone with our intellect and decision-making talents. Robots also lack the mixture of good and bad qualities that religion and philosophy define as "human."

But scientists and engineers want the next generations of useful robots to include advanced computers and artificial intelligence—to be smarter. They will make more decisions and they may seem more human. Already people are asking what the robots of the future will mean to our human skills, jobs, ethics, and freedoms. These are useful questions to keep in mind as you read the remainder of this book.

2 ANATOMY OF A ROBOT

Looking at one of today's working robots is not like looking into a mirror. But robots and people have a lot in common, inside, because robot design is based on the human body.

The Human Body—and a Robot's Body

The human body is like a team of experts. Each team member has a special skill that can be used in lots of different ways. Working together, the team can tackle many jobs under many conditions.

Two arms and two hands lift, hold, and work with things that are big or small, light or heavy, delicate or strong. Two legs and two feet can move a person along the sidewalk, up mountains, down into water, and through drifting sand or snow. Five senses monitor a person's environment. And the brain runs the whole operation.

Most robots are designed to do only one or two specific jobs. This is partly because scientists haven't figured out just how the human body does everything, or how to build a robot to work like a human. So a robot's "body team" is much simpler. Each robot has only the number of arms, hands, legs, senses, and other abilities it needs for its work. A computer runs all of a robot's operations. But human beings are still in ultimate control.

Arms and Hands

One of the great differences between humans and other species is that we can make and use lots of tools in lots of ways. A robot is the ultimate tool—one programmed to work independently. In fact, a robot is a system of tools. Its own most important tool is what people call its arm and hand. They are so important that they have their own branch on the robot family tree, the branch entitled "manipulators/machine tools."

First, a word about the terms *arm* and *hand*. Some scientists and engineers don't like these humanlike—or *anthropomorphic*—terms because robots aren't people. They use *manipulator* instead of *arm* and *end effector* instead of *hand*. This fits the idea of designing the robot for the task, materials, and environment.

Other scientists like *arm* and *hand*. They say that the human body is a good model for designing a robot and that once we have a good humanlike robot, later designs can become less "human." This was done in the past with airplane design, when birds were the inspiration. Early planes were much more birdlike than today's are.

The human arm and hand are made of up of several body tissues. Bones give them shape and structure. Joints, tendons, and cartilage let them extend, retract, and rotate. The skin contains environmental sensors. The nerves bring instructions from the brain and send sensory signals to the brain. And the muscles use electrical and mechanical energy to do the work of motion, lifting, and carrying.

Robot arms and hands imitate all these functions. Today's robot arm extends from a base (body) and is composed of rigid metal *links* that take the place of bone, tendons, and cartilage. It also has flexible *joints*—a "shoulder," a "wrist," and sometimes more. A computer, or *processor*, decides what to do; a motor or other *actuator* provides the muscle power. Sensors react to the environment. And electrical wiring carries messages between the computer and the arm and hand.

Arms

Some experts say that the blacksmith tongs found in ancient Egyptian tombs were the first manipulators. People have always used hand tongs of some sort to handle hot or hazardous materials. The next generation was a tong that could be extended and retracted.

The need to handle radioactive materials in the 1940s brought a great advance in manipulators. These materials required very precise handling, such as cutting, pouring, and assembling. But they were too dangerous to touch directly or even get close to. The problem was solved with development of the *master-slave manipulator*. With this equipment a person's (the *master*) arm and hand movements on a pair of handles were extended into a protective box containing the mate-

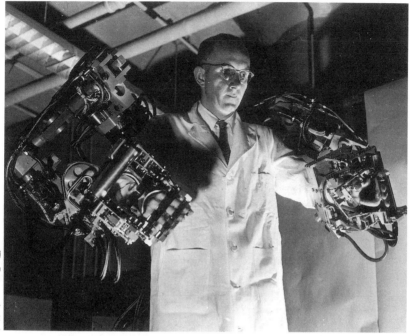

General Electric engineer Ralph Mosher manipulates a master control harness; a slave unit responds instantly with an exact duplication of Mosher's motions. This unit, called Handyman, was built for G.E.'s Aircraft Nuclear Propulsion Department to service radioactively "hot" components of a nuclear propulsion system for aircraft at an Atomic Energy Commission National Reactor Testing Station.

rials. The tool ends (the mechanical *slaves*) inside the box did the actual work.

At first, master-slave manipulators were powered entirely by human muscles. Then motors were added. They greatly increased the amount of work the slave end could do. Motors also allowed a greater distance between master and slave. In some cases, sensors at the slave end fed back information about operations to the master.

Computer control of the system was the next improvement. Commands were entered in a computer at the master end. They were sent to another computer that directed the actions of the slave. However, a person was still in control of the processing. The master could make changes in operations on the basis of personal observation.

In time, processing too was computerized. Now many details could be handled automatically. For example, once a manipulator was placed in position to loosen a bolt, a computer program could direct

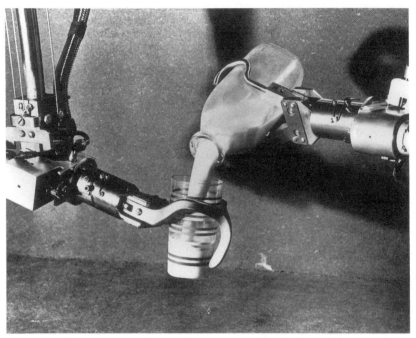

This 1948 photo shows mechanical hands pouring milk, but the hands were built to mix chemicals in experiments that had to be performed in radioactive areas.

the actual operation. This made the control system a two-level operation, or *hierarchy*. On the top level, a person directed overall operations, including decisionmaking. On the level below, the computer handled the simpler tasks.

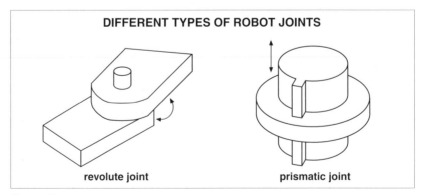

DIFFERENT TYPES OF ROBOT JOINTS

revolute joint   prismatic joint

Figure 2

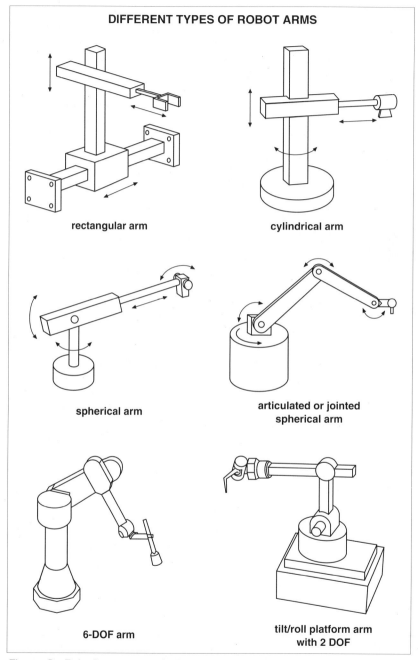

DIFFERENT TYPES OF ROBOT ARMS

rectangular arm

cylindrical arm

spherical arm

articulated or jointed
spherical arm

6-DOF arm

tilt/roll platform arm
with 2 DOF

Figure 3: Robotic arms are designed to move in various ways depending upon the function of the robot.

Two kinds of joint are commonly used. One type, called *revolute* or rotary, is similar to the human kind. Others, called *prismatic*, work by sliding, in which a link is moved in space like a sliding door. But it keeps its direction relative to the link at the other end of the joint—a movement called *translation*.

For a robotic arm to move, the controller program must calculate several positions and routes. One is from the hand's present location to the point where it will do its job. This requires movement at each joint. You can see how this works with your own arm and hand. Say you move your hand from this book to a can of soda pop. There are position changes at your elbow and your shoulder. For a robot to make this motion it must calculate the position change for each joint.

The flexibility of a robot arm is called its *degrees of freedom*, or DOF. Each joint is one degree of freedom. Commercial robots have from one to seven degrees of freedom. Experimental robots have as many as 20 DOF.

Muscle Power

A robot's arm is powered by an actuator at each joint. *Electric motors* are the most common type. *Pneumatic* (air pressure) and *hydraulic* (pressurized oil) systems are also used.

Pneumatically operated robots are modern versions of the 18th-century Flute Player. The robot's arms and legs are really cylinders and pistons (plungers)—like a hand-operated tire pump. Compressed air is pumped into a cylinder, moving the piston. This in turn provides the limb's motion. The airflow and the motion are computer controlled. Hydraulic systems work much the same way, but with a fluid instead of air.

Pneumatic and hydraulic types are reliable, but they can have problems. Their pumping systems have to be at a distance from the manipulator. Hydraulic systems can have the same problems that the family car does; lots of hoses, valves, and pumps increase the chance of oil leaks or seepage. Pneumatic systems are harder to use accurately, and air pressure can wear down the seals that keep air from escaping.

Hands

The human hand is marvelously flexible. From the main palm, each of four fingers is attached by a joint. Each finger has two joints of its own. Our two-jointed, opposable thumb is attached very close to the wrist, so it can move independently. People can form their hands into

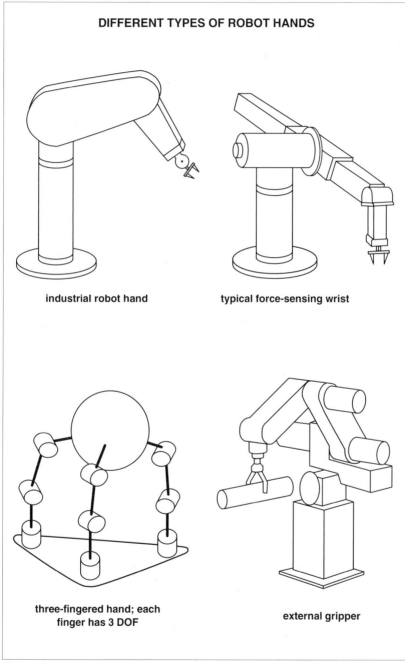

DIFFERENT TYPES OF ROBOT HANDS

industrial robot hand

typical force-sensing wrist

three-fingered hand; each
finger has 3 DOF

external gripper

Figure 4

many shapes, from making a tight fist to spreading it wide like a paddle, scoop, or net. And they can form various finger combinations for specific tasks, like picking up a feather, writing with a pencil, holding a softball, adjusting a microscope, or taking a sample of cake frosting to lick.

A robot's end effector has a very limited and specialized shape and function. *Grippers* are robot hands designed to grasp and hold. Some work like the human thumb and first finger. Others aren't humanlike at all—magnets and suction cups, for instance. Some robots have two or more grippers attached to the wrist.

Also, the gripper may be designed to best grasp a particular type of object. For example, some grippers grasp the object on the outside (*external grippers*). But if the part is ring-shaped, the gripper may be designed to hold it from the inside (*internal grippers*).

In some industrial work, a robot must use a series of tools. So the arm and hand must be designed to pick up a tool, use it, release it, and pick up another. If only one tool is required, it may be attached directly to the wrist. This is often the case with spray paint nozzles, welding torches, cutters, drills, brushes, grinders, and liquid cement applicators.

Moving Around

Robotic motion requires legs and feet, or substitutes. A mobile robot also must have a navigation system.

Legs and Feet

Most mobile robots don't walk on two humanlike legs. In fact, most don't have legs and feet at all. Two or four legs (or wheels) may seem "right" to us, because that's what mammals use, but they're not very stable. Three-legged stools are always stable, even when the legs aren't the same length. A four-legged table almost always wobbles a little. Many insects use six legs, often keeping three on the ground at the same time, for stability. Many robots have sets of three, four, six, or more wheels.

Others move on treads or tracks, which are really a set of wheels running inside an endless pathway. Some robots have two tracks; others use four.

A few robotic leg systems have been designed but most aren't in practical use. An exception is the pneumatically operated four-leg system developed by Dinamation International Corp. that moves

(Official U.S. Navy photograph)

This 1983 photo shows a six-legged walker robot at the Naval Surface Weapons Center.

life-sized figures of dinosaurs and other prehistoric animals for educational and entertainment displays.

The *pantograph*—a series of adjustable parallelograms—was invented in the 18th century for copying graphics in various sizes. It was later adapted for grasping objects on high shelves and was widely used in grocery stores. In the 1970s, the 3-D pantograph—one that can move in three dimensions—was invented. It is now used for robot arms, fingers, and legs.

A huge three-ton research robot built by Ohio State University uses six hydraulically powered pantograph legs to walk and climb over steep obstacles. Balance sensors and vision help the controller to choose the robot's path. The 3-D pantographs make the legs extremely flexible. Force sensors allow adjustable pressure. The legs can crush a large piece of machinery or move a fragile box.

Whether the "legs" carry a dinosaur or perform a special task, the design problems are the same. The legs must support the weight of the robot's body and its load. And they must allow the most stable motion, especially over ramps, stairs, or uneven ground, or when carrying large or bulky loads.

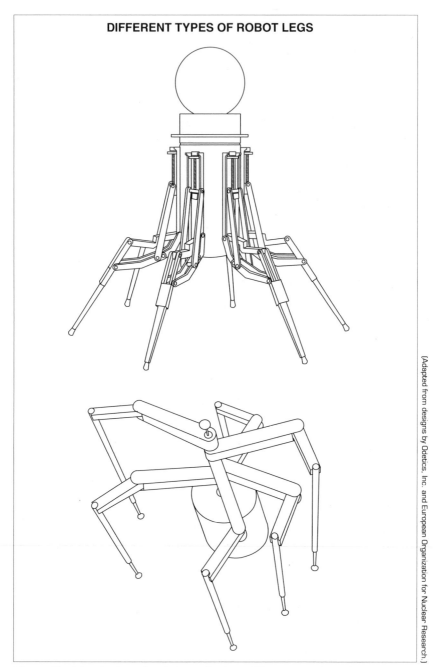

DIFFERENT TYPES OF ROBOT LEGS

[Adapted from designs by Odetics, Inc. and European Organization for Nuclear Research.]

Figure 5: Two designs for six-legged robots. The upper robot climbs steps and avoids obstacles. The lower robot moves on a level surface.

Made by Dinamation, this hands-on model, called a Dimetrodon, shows the robotic legs, which can be moved with a joy stick.

Navigation

A person might describe where he or she lives this way: "I live north of the shopping mall. It takes about 10 minutes to drive there in normal traffic." Possibly without realizing it, this person has just used a system of navigation called *dead reckoning*.

Navigation—getting from where one is to where one wants to go—can be an exact science. Today ships and airplanes can rely on star atlases, satellite signals, weather indicators, directional compasses, and other equipment to sail from New York to London or to fly from New York to Denver. The same equipment can guide a spaceship from Cape Canaveral to the moon or farther.

Before the 15th century, dead reckoning—navigating by knowing only speed and direction—was state-of-the-art. But even with today's tools, dead reckoning has its place—for very short trips, such as those a mobile robot might make from one room to another or into a hazardous environment. Its accuracy depends on knowing three things: exactly how fast one is going, what one's direction is, and how long one has been moving. If a person, or a robot, makes a mistake in any of them, he, she, or it will soon be lost.

One might think that moving from one place to another within a building would be an easy navigation problem. But any obstacle can

(Courtesy of Prof. Kenneth J. Waldron, Ohio State University)

The pantograph robot built by Ohio State University.

throw the mover off-course, like having to detour around a trash can or bumping into a chair that's out of place. As a practical matter, most mobile robots in daily use follow electronic signals embedded in the floor.

Navigation and other robot actions involve interaction with the environment. People know about their environment because of their five senses. Robots have sensors for the same reason.

Sensors

Sensors are robotic versions of the human senses. Robots can have sensors that imitate the functions of four of our senses: cameras for vision, acoustical arrays for hearing, smoke and gas detectors for smell, and force and *torque* (twisting) sensors for touch. Robots aren't big on eating, so there are no taste sensors. But they can have thermometers, to keep track of environmental temperatures.

Vision

Vision systems are useful for mobile robots and for those that pick up, assemble, shape, or cut materials. Cameras play the role of the human iris, lens, and retina. They use visible light to take pictures in black-and-white or color.

Visible Light

Of course, taking the picture isn't the same as knowing what it means. When a person looks at something, the brain gives the image its meaning. The retina passes the image—a set of light waves that bounce off objects—to rods and cones in the back of the eye. Interpretation of the image starts with them. They tell dark from light and one color from another. They pass the information on to a part of the brain called the *visual cortex*, for final *image analysis*.

This includes recognizing patterns, which are shapes that occur over and over. Boundaries are important too. There are also building edges, lines that separate light and dark areas, and distinct objects within one's field of vision. Using three dimensions with our side-by-side eyes also helps us understand what we're seeing. Using only one eye makes patterns, boundaries, and objects harder to recognize.

The flat 2-D image from one eye is fine for picking up a pencil from a table. But telling how close someone is standing to a grove of trees requires depth, or 3-D, vision.

But image analysis also has many uncertainties. Is that tall, dark object a tree or a telephone pole? Is that line a boundary between sidewalk and grass? Or is it the edge of a high wall? Are those rippling patterns a pond surface or a wheat field? Is that short, bulky object in the corner a trash bin or an air-conditioning unit?

To answer these questions, the brain must compare its first analysis with what it already knows. Memory holds past experience, plus what one has learned from books, pictures, and what one has heard. The brain uses these memories to decide what the person is seeing and what, if anything, he or she should do in response.

Two people looking at a scene may not agree on what they see. One person may think the bulky object is an air-conditioning unit, while the other thinks it's a trash bin. Each person made a decision based on incomplete or uncertain information. After discussion, one of the observers may have a change of mind about the scene, or else decide more information is needed.

For a robot's vision system, the camera supplies the image. This is often a *CCD*, or charge-coupled device, which uses a light-sensitive computer chip instead of film. The brain power and image analysis come from a computer. A robot's vision analysis program is much simpler than a person's. Most robots can't deal with uncertainties the way a person's eye and brain can.

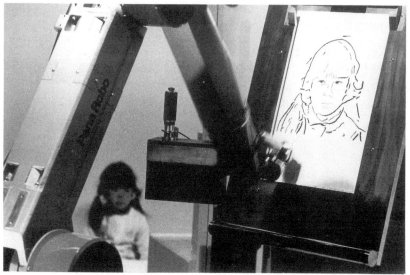

Some robot vision systems make it seem almost as if the robot can see. This robot, on display at Matsushita Pavilion at the International Exposition 1985, can draw visitors' portraits with a brush in less than three minutes.

A robot on the job must make yes-no decisions. Is the assembly piece in the right place to have a hole drilled in it? Is it close enough to pick up? Most industrial robots that "see" have two-dimensional, black-and-white vision systems. And they can't move over to get a better look.

Mobile robots usually have some three-dimensional vision. And some of them can see in color. They need 3-D and color because their vision is part of their navigational system—just as a person's is. Not only are they moving, but some of the people or objects they see may be moving too.

Other Electromagnetic Radiation

Other portions of the electromagnetic spectrum besides visible light can also be used to take a picture. Some robotic eyes can "see" infrared or heat waves. Infrared waves come from living people and animals and from objects that are warmer than their surroundings. This is useful at night or where the light level is very low. Some robots are equipped with X-ray systems.

Touch, Force, and Torque Sensors

One of the most advanced touch sensing systems ever developed is the fingertips and palm of the human hand. This system contains four kinds of organ to sense shapes and textures. It has 17,000 sensors. They work by detecting changes in the skin, such as stretching and pressure. Then they trigger nerve cells, which pass the information to the brain's *somatosensory cortex* for processing. Touching this book, for example, will activate them.

The "fingerprint" creases and ridges—the fingertip pads—contain two types of organ. When sliding a hand down a side of the book, one type of organ senses its edges, size, and shape. Rubbing the finger pads over the book page activates the other type of organ, which is also found in the palm. It provides information about the page's texture. Pressing a hand down on the book activates a third type of organ, telling how rigid or flexible the surface is. Finally, stretching the fingers out flat makes the skin vibrate and activates the fourth type of touch organ.

Robots aren't always accurate. The design, the materials they're made of, and heat and other environmental conditions can cause navigational errors. Robots need touch sensors to tell the controlling computer whether the robot hand is actually where it should be. The controller must calculate the difference between where the robot actually is and where it's supposed to be. Then it sends a command to correct the error.

Scientists haven't yet been able to develop a material as flexible and sensitive as human skin. But they have developed sensors that can tell how an object's shape and contour respond to compression (force) and distortion (torque, or twisting motions).

Position can be sensed on the actuator by one of several devices. The sensors measure changes in electronic signals caused by rotation of the motor's shaft. The two most common types are the *incremental rotary optical encoder* and the *resolver*.

The human hand can control force very precisely. For instance, it allows just the right amount to grip an egg, which is different from the amount needed to hold a tennis ball. Still another amount of force may be required to hold the aluminum cap of a soda pop bottle and twist it off. Too strong a grip will bend the cap out of shape. But a much stronger grip may be needed to twist a steel nut from a bolt.

Assembling materials, drilling holes, and lifting objects are common robot jobs. The robot must use the right amounts of force and torque for the material. Those amounts are designed into the robot and its computer program for each job.

Force and torque are usually measured at the hand end with *strain gauges*. These contain semiconductors that produce signals that get stronger as more force or torque is used.

Sensing Sound, Odor, and Heat

When a bat flies through the night air, it emits high-pitched sounds that echo back after bouncing off trees, buildings, and other objects. Whales and porpoises use similar systems under water. Sounds like this are called *sonar* (*so*und *na*vigation and *r*anging). Sonar has long been used for ship navigation and submarine detection. It is the basis for some self-focusing cameras. And it is also used by mobile robots.

Sound is a disruption of the air or water that is expressed as waves of energy. Like light, sound waves can be reflected by objects they strike. The distance between a sound source and its target can be measured by the amount of time required for the echo to return. A robot can use sonar to tell how far it is from a wall or doorway.

Robots may also be equipped with smoke and gas detectors or thermometers.

The Brain

The human brain is a real jack-of-all-trades. It's the captain of a person's "body team," controlling all the operations. It can take totally new information, analyze it, find memories (stored information) for comparison. It combines the information in new ways. And it learns from the experience. If it has to, the brain can act immediately on its new knowledge and then store the whole thing for future use. In computer terms, it maintains a data, or knowledge, base and performs information processing.

People's brains guide their interactions with their world in several ways. It learns, it stores knowledge, and by staying in constant touch with the world, it can plan people's actions and tell them how to react second by second. A robot has to know its world, too, in order to interact with it.

A Robot's World

Each person has a personal world that is a part of the larger world. A student's world is made up of familiar areas—home, neighborhood, bus route, school, park—and the student interacts just with those parts that the senses can detect and the information that the brain can process.

Each species senses and understands its personal world differently. A human sees in a wide range of colors. A dog or cat sees mostly in black and white. A person immediately recognizes a blowing leaf by its shape. But a cat may see it as a threat. At night, a human sees darkness, but a cat sees distinct objects. The air that sounds quiet to a human may be full of sounds for a dog.

A robot moves in a world, too. Its world is limited by its design, the materials it's made of, its sensors, and its programming. A robot's controller program has to store a picture or word-picture of that world. It also must know how the robot should interact with the world. It must keep up-to-date information about the way it's actually interacting. And it must be able to send instructions to correct any errors.

Putting It Together in the Real World

Suppose a softball player is at bat in a game. Several experts in that person's "body team" are taking part. The eyes are at work watching the ball. They send a stream of information to the brain about the ball's speed, height, and perhaps the way it is turning. At the same time, the brain is evaluating this information. It is also controlling the way the person stands at the plate and calculating how the ball should be hit.

At the instant the ball reaches the plate, the brain decides whether the batter should swing or let the ball go by. If the brain selects swinging, it sends "how to move" messages to the arms, upper body, and legs. If it made the right decision, the batter hits the ball. In that case, the brain sends further messages, instructing the hands to drop the bat and the legs to streak to first base.

Sometimes the brain miscalculates, and the batter swings, but misses. In such a case, the brain adds this experience to its memory to help make a better decision next time.

The brain has been working on several problems at the same time—what is called *parallel processing*. The human brain is very good at this. For instance, at the same time the batter's brain was deciding about the pitched ball, it was also making sure the person's heart was beating, telling the intestines to continue the digestion process, and directing every other body function.

Some of these tasks are so routine that the person doesn't realize they're happening. Other tasks require advanced processing. Making decisions and controlling operations are very complicated chores. There are lots of facts and lots of uncertainties. So the brain also works on several levels at once, a *hierarchy*.

Most computers can do only one job at a time, what is called *serial* processing. They're very good at processing numbers. In fact, they can do that much faster than the human brain can. But a robot may have several tasks to do at the same time. In this case, it needs a different serial computer for each task.

The computer controlling a robot's overall operations and making decisions is a lot like a personal computer. It sits on a desk and has a screen and a keyboard. Other robot computers are single-purpose ("*dedicated*") microprocessors (computer chips). There is a different chip for motion and guidance, sensor data processing, sound, speech, and other functions. They all work together, so the effect is brainlike.

Robot School—Teaching Robots To Be Robots

Factory robots must be taught to do the useful work, such as assembling a product or carrying an object from one place to another. The teacher first has to know the robot's abilities: how it learns and how much it can be taught. For instance, the teacher must know what the robot's arms can do. Industrial robots have either *fixed-stop* or *servo-controlled* arms.

Fixed-stop Robots

A fixed-stop arm is like a train that stops only at its stations, never in between. The arms of fixed-stop robots can stop only at preset points on the *work path*. This is the route the arm or each link takes from its starting point until it reaches the work location.

If a robot has fixed stops, it can learn only the sequence of moves. Robots of this type are used for simple *pick-and-place* operations. A person can teach one to pick up a finished item from a worktable, turn, then place the item on a conveyor belt.

Servo-controlled

A servo-controlled robot has more abilities. A *servomechanism* is a device that knows where a joint or arm is, in relation to its possible range. It feeds this information back to the control program. This lets the controller compare where the arm should be, and how fast it's moving, with its real position and speed. Once it knows this, the controller can stop the arm anywhere along its work path.

There are also two methods for controlling servo robots' movements. Some robots have *point-to-point* control. This means that the robot can stop only at points it has already been taught. This type of robot is used for assembly tasks. For instance, it can go to a storage area, retrieve a part or tool, return to its workplace, and perform a task. It can go through this sequence of motions many times. Any errors that creep in can be adjusted by the controller.

Other robots have *continuous path* control. Only the beginning and end points of a motion are set. Such robots perform work with a moving arm, such as painting a car body or welding two pieces of metal. The arm can "learn" by being guided through its motion, or the controller can calculate the actual path and any in-between stopping points.

Most industrial robots take only straight paths. More advanced robots can also take curved paths.

Teaching Methods

Someone must teach a robot what movements to make and when to make them. The process is much like teaching someone to dance or roller skate.

There are two ways to teach a robot. A human teacher can move the arm through the motion, recording each start and stop position with a control box called a *teach pendant.* This is called *lead-through* programming. Once all the movements are recorded, the robot can repeat them at work. This kind of robot is called a *playback* or *record and playback* robot.

Other robots can be programmed using a computer language specially designed to describe motions and angles. Most "simple" human motions are quite complex and difficult to describe. For instance, to pour a glass of juice from a pitcher requires grasping the handle of the pitcher, lifting it, and tilting it. The arm must move and hold the pitcher at a precise angle. When the glass is full, the pitcher must be tilted and set back down, again by moving the arm and changing angles.

To program a robot to do the same thing requires a language that tells the robot when and how far to move, grasp and release, and change the angle of one or more joints. Some of the languages also take sensor readings, so the robot will stop, for instance, if pressure on an object is too great. (In fact, pouring a glass of juice is beyond the abilities of today's robots.)

The latest teaching method is *graphics-based programming.* It combines record-and-playback and programming. A computer simulation of the robot in action is created. The simulation is programmed with the work sequence. Motion and programming errors are corrected on the simulated robot. Then the final version of the program is transferred to the real robot's controller.

From Master-Slave to Androids

Some of today's robots have very little independence. Others have a a lot. Some are remotely controlled by a human operator, what is called a *teleoperated* device. They're direct descendants of the basic master-slave manipulators. Teleoperation provides very precise and realistic operations, almost as if the operator were performing the operations directly.

- An *intelligent teleoperated* system has some computerized control at the slave or remote end.
- With *supervised autonomy*, the robot's computer performs almost all the decision making as well as calculations, but a human can still take control of either operations or decision making.
- The *fully autonomous* robot is completely free of human control.

Some people might think that the more independent robots perform the most complex or sophisticated tasks. Despite the impression given by science fiction androids, this is not necessarily true for today's robots. For instance, some of today's most sophisticated tasks, such as undersea exploration, are performed with intelligent teleoperated systems, which are also called *telerobots*.

We haven't progressed to fully autonomous robots yet, let alone androids that would look and behave like humans. But in the next chapters you will see the other robot types at work today.

3 ROBOTS AT WORK TODAY

Right now, robots are a part of our lives, perhaps more than we think. TV sets are often made by robots. The office mail in large companies is sometimes delivered by robots. Nuclear power produces electricity in many areas, and robots perform maintenance work on the reactors. The family car undoubtedly bears the robotic touch: parts welded together, the windshield installed, the body painted. One can even buy a pint-sized security robot to patrol the house when nobody's home.

There are almost 40,000 robots at work in the United States, and many more around the world. And the number is growing.

When robots first came on the scene, people thought each robot would be a general worker. They thought a robot would be able to use many tools to do lots of tasks. Things didn't work out that way. Each type of job was too specialized. And even the same job turned out to be very different in different plants. Experience has shown that robots must specialize. Each model must be designed for a single purpose. Even then, it often must be adapted to the environment it will be working in.

Some robots are designed for industrial manufacturing. They are very different from robots used in hazardous environments, delivery and other services, and security. Most robots today are found in factories.

Factory Robots

In the United States, industrial robots are used chiefly in the auto industry. By themselves or teamed with machine tools, robots also work in general manufacturing. They drill and cut. They assemble and spray paint. They load and unload materials. They inspect.

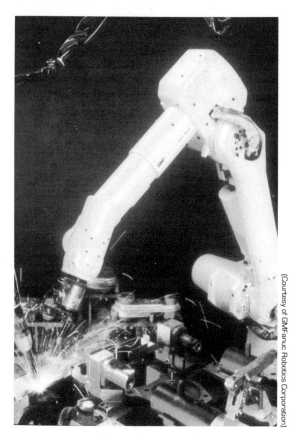

An arc welding robot

(Courtesy of GMFanuc Robotics Corporation)

'Robots are also being used in new and different manufacturing processes. Do you have a pair of pre-faded jeans in your closet? A robot may have added the well-worn look.

In many cases, robots are used in traditional factories. But they have had only limited success. To be useful, industrial robots must be part of an overall automated and flexible system, controlled by computers. Such flexible manufacturing systems now exist.

Flexible Manufacturing Systems

In the 1980s they were called "factories of the future." Now the future is here. An auto maker in Tennessee, a computer maker in California, and many manufacturing plants worldwide have become *flexible*

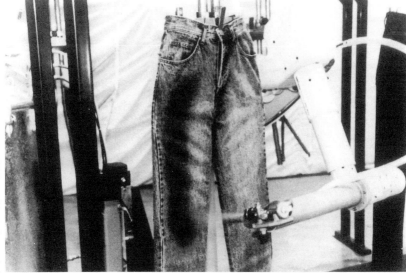

A robot makes new blue jeans look fashionably old with a local abrasion process.

manufacturing systems. The systems are sometimes called *computer integrated manufacturing,* or CIM.

Actual product-making is just a part of factory automation, even with robots at work. The finished product has to be designed. Raw materials must be ordered, stockpiled, and kept track of. The manufacturing process must be planned, so it is accurate and efficient. Production and sales must be coordinated, so there aren't too many items to sell or too few for the customers. Finally, plant managers and owners need an accounting system. This keeps track of the money spent and, hopefully, the profits.

Most of these tasks are done on computers. The ordering department has its own computer system. The design department has one also, and so do the sales and accounting departments. But suppose all these computer systems were linked into one big system. And suppose the system also tied into the manufacturing and assembly process, including robots. There might even be automated carts and conveyor belts to get parts and materials from storage and move them between work areas.

Suppose a manufacturer has brought out one of its products in a new color. The sales department learns that the new color isn't selling very well, but people are buying so many of another product that all the store shelves are empty. The factory line could quickly shift from

(Courtesy of Nissan Motor Manufacturing Corporation USA)

A flexible manufacturing system is installed at Nissan.

the new color item to the one that the stores are asking for. With a computer-integrated system, raw material orders could be changed, robots reprogrammed, and dollars kept track of, all at the same time. It would also be fairly easy to gear up for a new and improved item.

In traditional car-making, for instance, a change of models from one year to the next takes almost a year. A large plant may have a thousand or more record-and-playback robots. Each one must be reprogrammed by hand. The changeover itself is costly. And an idle assembly line means products that aren't being made and sold.

Nissan Motor Corp. has installed flexible manufacturing systems in several of its plants, including one in Smyrna, Tennessee. The old manufacturing system needed specialized tools to handle the parts for each car model. Changing models meant changing all these tools. The heart of Nissan's flexible system is a team of robots that can grip and weld any body parts from any of the company's car models.

After the work is done, still other sensor-equipped robots inspect it for accuracy. Information about manufacturing errors is fed back to the computers. Programming is then changed automatically, so work on the next piece is more accurate.

To switch models, only the robots' programming has to be changed. The company says this cuts the model changeover time to just a few months, and the costs are reduced by 80 percent.

In traditional car-making, design of the production process doesn't start until the product's design is complete. With a flexible system, the product and the manufacturing process can be designed at the same time. By the time the product is ready to be made, the automated assembly line is also ready to go to work.

Flexible manufacturing systems are also used for products much smaller than automobiles—like computers. NeXT Computer, Inc.'s manufacturing plant in California uses a computer-and-robot system for the entire production process, from design to shipment.

NeXT says that its flexible system prevented costly manufacturing delays. It also allows rapid changes in production, if necessary. And it provided a very accurate working product—a result of what is called quality assurance.

[Courtesy of NeXT Computer, Inc.]

NeXT uses a computer and robot flexible manufacturing system to make computer chips.

Service Industry

The service industries—those that provide a service to consumers, rather than a product—are using robots in many places, sometimes where you wouldn't expect them. Robots are becoming part of the service work team in restaurants and food service operations, equipment maintenance and floor care, and mail and delivery. For example, the U.S. Postal Service has added floor-cleaning robots to six large mail-handling facilities. The robots are cost-effective for the large floor areas involved.

In fact, robots are generally most useful in large operations, where they can do routine work, while people take on more specialized jobs. Mail carts and material delivery systems are widely used examples. Delivery carts are also used in automated warehouses, where most of the work is done by conveyor belt systems, elevators, and almost-robotic carts. At least one large hospital uses a fully robotic cart system for its deliveries.

Robot Delivery Systems

Most people think of hospitals as places where sick people get well and where women have babies. This, of course, is part of their purpose. But in its operation, a hospital is a big delivery system. Medications and supplies must be delivered from storage to nursing stations and operating rooms. Clean sheets and towels must appear regularly in patients' rooms. Soiled instruments and other leftovers must be taken to the laundry or the trash. Food—regular meals and special diets—must be delivered on time from the central kitchen to the patients. Afterward the trays of dirty dishes must be removed.

In many hospitals, it's common to see heavy trays of food or linen baskets being hand-pushed onto elevators and then into public corridors. It used to be that way at the U.S. Navy's Balboa Hospital in San Diego. But in the mid-1980s, a new and larger hospital was built, and robots were designed into it. Instead of human power, robotic carts deliver supplies and food. They pick up soiled laundry and used trays. But you never see them in the elevators and corridors. This is because the hospital has separate corridors and elevators just for the robots. Following electronic pathways placed beneath the flooring, robots move through the hospital.

The three-wheeled robots look much like golf carts. They are powered by four 12-volt batteries and can carry as much as 500 pounds.

Robotic carts in their own corridor at U.S. Naval Hospital

The heart of the system is the computer control room, complete with map, that keeps track of all the carts. Dispatchers use keypads at "robot stops" to summon a cart to a pickup point. The cart positions itself under a basket of supplies or a tray of food, raises its back platform to lift the rack off the floor, and goes to its destination. Once the cart gets its instructions, it moves slowly—about a half-mile per hour—through a robot corridor. It takes a robots-only elevator to the correct floor.

Radio-frequency signals transmitted through guidepaths buried in the floor provide all the commands to receptors located underneath the carts. Clusters of magnets buried in the floor generate magnetic fields that open or close switches on the cart, allowing it to send or receive certain types of signals. These include "go to an elevator," "switch to a different radio frequency," "turn," "go in another direction," or "unload."

Programming and signals from touch and optical distance sensors keep robots from moving too close together. A cart will stop if it bumps into something. The optical sensors detect differences in light levels. The carts are highly reflective, and if a sensor picks up a high light level, it will issue a stop signal.

Each floor in the hospital has special rooms that connect to both the robot and the human corridors. Only certain employees are admitted. Otherwise, no one sees either the robots or their travel lanes. When a cart stops at a "robot stop" outside the room, an authorized employee unloads the cart and sends it on its way. Only then are the supplies and food distributed through the human corridors. Trash, empty food trays, and other throwaways follow the same route, only in reverse.

Working in Hazardous Environments

Electric transmission lines, nuclear power plants, and coal mining all supply the energy our homes and factories need. Many people make their livings in the energy industry, but it can be a dangerous work environment. Workers wear protective clothing. And there are rules about how much exposure they are allowed. Even so, some jobs are so dangerous that robots are being used instead of people.

Today robots are used in the nuclear industry. They also help police get rid of bombs. When there's a toxic chemical spill, robots take part in the cleanup. They work in coal mines and they fight fires. Some have been designed for the construction industry.

They are designed for specific tasks so there is great variation in how they look. Some are huge. One looks like a giant earth-moving machine. Others are tiny. One looks like a snake. Another looks like a six-wheeled roller skate.

Nuclear Reactor Inspection

The inside of a nuclear power reactor is filled with pipes and tanks that carry radioactive hot water or steam. A combination of radiation and aging can damage reactor parts. This could cause a leakage of radioactive materials into the environment. Reactor operators must inspect the reactor's insides constantly. Since the radioactive environment is too dangerous for people to work in, robots are used instead. Some robots patrol the interior of the reactor, inspecting for pipe leaks. Some robots are small enough to roll or climb inside pipes that are only six inches in diameter. Robots can carry out inspections using video or sonar. Or they can take gamma ray pictures (like medical X rays). A few have sound sensors that "listen" to the pipes. Strange noises can mean that a pipe should be replaced or bypassed.

Others retrieve tools or additional materials left behind during construction or repairs. Some are equipped with environmental sensors. They measure the air temperature, humidity, and radiation level.

Robots make repairs inside the reactors. And they clean walls, change filters, clean up contaminated pipes and other areas, and remove sludge. Some can even turn valves on and off.

TOMCAT—Live Electric Transmission Line Maintenance

The lines that transmit electricity can be a very dangerous working environment. Workers must be protected against the electricity. They work high off the ground on towers or trucks with lifts. They cannot work during high winds or lightning, or when it is very hot or very cold. Even when conditions are right, the workers must carry heavy equipment to the lines with them. Then they perform delicate repairs and maintenance, such as changing insulators. And they do it while wearing heavy gloves and other clothing to protect them from the electric current.

Now a robot named TOMCAT can do the work of a six-person crew. TOMCAT stands for **T**eleoperator for **O**perations, **M**aintenance, and **C**onstruction Using **A**dvanced **T**echnology. It handles lines and makes repairs.

Coal Mining

Coal mining is one of the most hazardous work environments in all industry. For this reason, robots are being developed to work effi-

[Courtesy of U.S. Bureau of Mines]

A coal-mining robot at work

(Courtesy of U.S. Bureau of Mines)

Technicians operating the remote control of a coal-mining robot

ciently in coal seams deep underground. Some robots can work for long stretches of time, either remotely operated or with an operator in an attached cab. One robot miner is being tested by the U.S. Bureau of Mines. It can work as far as 1,000 feet from its control station. The operator uses the robot's vision system to help control its movements.

Security Robots

Almost all office buildings, stores, and factories have security systems. These are human guards, video camera systems, wall-mounted alarms, or a combination of systems. Good security systems are expensive. Guards can't be everywhere at once. Video cameras and wall alarms aren't always successful in detecting intruders or other problems. A sentry robot to patrol the building can be an added security tool.

A sentry robot is a special type of mobile robot. Besides navigating through its environment, it must have sensors and programming to tell normal from unusual conditions.

When a robot patrols the corridors, its sensors tell it that things are normal, such as office furniture being where it should be, corridor lights turned on but office lights off, and the building's temperature at 68 degrees. The robot notes a few ordinary abnormalities, such as the wastebaskets in a different place.

The robot is also programmed to observe out-of-the-ordinary abnormalities, such as a corridor temperature much higher than normal or smoke in the air. These conditions can cause the robot to sound a fire alarm. If the temperature is too low, it could mean an open outer door. The robot can tell if lights are on where they shouldn't be. Under these conditions, the robot may give an intruder alarm.

Security robots need many sensors. Besides light and temperature, they need infrared or light sensors for people or animals. Detectors are needed for smoke and gas. Water detectors respond to flooding from a leaking roof or a broken water pipe. Sound detectors hear footsteps, breaking glass, or voices. Vibration detectors locate doors being forced or blown open. Ultrasound systems find unexpected

(Courtesy of Denning Mobile Robots Inc.)

A sentry robot from Denning

obstacles, perhaps equipment or products being removed. The robot may also need radiation detectors.

The detectors must work together as a system, with one backing up another's findings. This is because the robot's controller should not make a judgment based on single occurrences. For instance, home smoke detectors sometimes go off while food is being cooked, after a certain concentration of smoke. It is easy to check immediately to be sure that no fire hazard is involved.

A robotic security system makes a sure judgment by having several types of sensor back each other up. For instance, if the noise and vibration sensors go off at the same time, someone may be trying to break in. Vision, motion, and heat detectors may all have to be set off, to indicate an intruder in the halls.

A higher heat level may mean that someone is in the room. But there is a difference between an unauthorized person and, for example, a mouse. The controller may be set to sound an alarm if the heat radiation is high enough to indicate a person, but not a mouse. It may also compare what the sensors have detected with past patterns. If conditions are above normal patterns, the computer signals building security or telephones for the police.

Security robots are not just for offices and factories. At least one is available for patrolling at home, ready to sound an alarm or call the police in case of intrusion.

Underwater Robots

The oceans cover two-thirds of the Earth's surface. They can be hostile and dangerous to humans. But the oceans contain forms of life, natural resources, and treasures from the past that people want. Until the 1950s, the ocean depths were visited only by a handful of scientists and adventurers, wearing heavy and clumsy old-fashioned diving suits or in hard-to-maneuver diving chambers.

Then, the ocean floor became an important source of petroleum. Oil companies needed to install and service huge offshore oil platforms and pipelines. New lightweight machines were developed to dive beneath the ocean's surface. Since robots were being developed at the same time, the two technologies were teamed up.

The military was one of the earliest users of undersea robots. The U.S. Navy used them to locate lost missiles. They even found a hydrogen bomb lost from a U.S. warplane off the coast of Spain.

[Navy photograph by PH2 (DV) William Curtsinger]

In this 1970 photo, the U.S. Navy submersible Nemo *makes a test dive in the Atlantic Ocean.*

By the late 1970s over 100 undersea vehicles were working in offshore oil fields around the world. Today there are too many to count. Besides the oil industry, they are used by marine biologists, archaeologists, mineral prospectors, and oceanographers. Environmental protection is another use. For example, robots have been used to investigate oil tanker accidents and discover how much oil has leaked from the ship and how much ecological damage has occurred. Even the tourist industry uses them to take visitors to underwater habitats.

Finding sunken treasure is another use for robots. They have been used to find sunken ships, ranging from 16th-century Spanish ships filled with gold to the ocean liner S.S. *Titanic*, which went down in 1912.

Undersea vehicles come in two major types. *Submersibles* are really small submarines. Some carry small crews or passenger groups. Larger vehicles are the underwater equivalent of tour buses, carrying as many as 48 passengers. *Remotely operated vehicles* (*ROVs*) have no crew or passengers. They are connected by communication lines to ships or platforms.

Not all underwater vehicles are robots, but many have such robotic features as manipulators with from 3 to 7 degrees of freedom, specialized end effectors, feedback sensors, and vision systems.

The Submersible *Alvin*

Alvin is famous as the submersible that found both the lost H-bomb and the *Titanic.* It has been used since 1964 for scientific research by the Woods Hole Oceanographic Institution in Massachusetts. One of its most interesting scientific discoveries was of colonies of tube worms and other organisms living near hot water vents deep on the ocean floor.

The 18-ton vehicle is operated by a pilot and can carry two other people on three-day missions. *Alvin* can dive as deep as 13,000 feet—a depth at which no unprotected human diver could survive.

Alvin has two hydraulic manipulators that are controlled by the ship's pilot to lift and carry. One arm has 6 DOF and can lift about 200 pounds. The other arm has 7 DOF and position feedback and can lift 250 pounds. For safety, the arms can be released from the inside and discarded, if necessary. Specialized end effectors can grasp or cut objects, take samples of the ocean floor, and place markers.

Remotely Operated Vehicles (ROVs)

Remotely operated vehicles—ROVs—have other functions. They can be used to dig a trench, take a soil sample, or lay and bury a communications cable or pipeline on the ocean floor. They can also inspect a ship hull or service an oil wellhead.

Most ROVs are controlled from ships or oil platforms through cables or *tethers*, which carry computer signals, pictures, and usually electric power. A few have their own power supplies but receive information through the tether. Some lack tethers and are controlled by TV signals. (ROVs of this type are sometimes called "autonomous," though they are not.)

Some ROVs are designed to swim in the water at specified depths. Others work on the ocean floor, either in a fixed position or mobile, able to crawl across the bottom on tracks.

In 1990, the communications company AT&T used bottom-crawling robots to lay fiber-optic cables across the Atlantic and Pacific oceans and the Caribbean Sea. The new cables will be used for high-speed data transmission as well as voice phone calls.

One Japanese robot called MARCAS (**MA**rine **R**obot for **C**able work **A**ssistance and **S**urveillance, made by KDD Laboratories) can test soil samples, detect problems in buried communications cables, and dig the cables up and repair them. The robot has black-and- white and color vision systems, sonar, one 7-DOF and one 5-DOF servo-controlled arm, and special cable grippers and cutters.

Another robot called Aquarobot (designed by the Japanese Ministry of Transport) can walk across the sea bottom on six spider-type legs at 6 feet per minute.

Deep Ocean Technology, Inc.'s Bandit robot services oil well-heads—the place on the ocean floor where the well meets the base of the platform structure. It inspects, cuts, and replaces parts using two 6-DOF arms, force and touch sensor feedback, and a lighted TV system to view its work area. Bandit uses the platform structure as its pathway.

Medicine and Health

Robots are at work in the medical sciences. They have assisted in surgery on both people and animals. In a California hospital, a robotic arm was used in several cases of brain surgery to measure the angle for entering the skull. Then the robotic arm held the drill as it worked. In a veterinary clinic, doctors used a robot to drill a hole in an elderly dog's leg bone so an artificial joint could be inserted. The patients recovered very well in all the operations. The surgeons said that the robots allowed much more precise drilling than with handheld methods.

Robotic exoskeletons—skeletons on the outside of the body—have also been tried to help partially paralyzed people to walk. Wearing the computer-controlled exoskeletons like boots, people have been able to walk limited distances. Other experiments are working toward robotic artificial hands, arms, and legs. Robotic wheelchairs are also under development.

Robots are being used in laboratories also. For example, Japanese scientists are using robots to analyze and identify DNA, the body's genetic material. The robots are part of a computerized and automated laboratory production line that works unattended around the clock. They transfer laboratory dishes and other equipment from one ana-lyzing machine to another. The automated equipment performs all the analysis, then transfers the information to the computer for storage.

Why Aren't There More Robots at Work?

In the mid-1980s, it was predicted that the use and manufacture of robots would increase greatly over the next few years. That has not happened. In fact, sales of robots went down.

The reason, one expert has said, is that robotics is like ice-skating. It's harder than it looks. Two problems are holding robotics back. Robots are not accurate enough. And they need greater intelligence.

For industrial robots, accuracy means getting the hand in just the right position. One study has found that most robots can get within only 0.6 inch of the target.

Accuracy involves the metal an arm is made of and the arm's speed. When metal moves, it vibrates. The faster the arm moves or the more it is extended, the more it vibrates. An arm cannot begin working until it stops vibrating. And vibration also disrupts the arm's path, so that it doesn't always end up on target. The problem is to move the arm quickly to the target without too much vibration.

The force and torque of the end effector at work can also affect accuracy; so can the softness or stiffness of the work material, friction at arm joints and as work is performed, and changes in temperature and humidity. Even gravity plays a role —the weight of the arm itself and the weight of what it is lifting.

Two ways engineers are trying to improve accuracy are by developing better control of motion and speed and better use of sensory feedback.

Robots also need to be "smarter." What does "intelligence" mean in robotics? The next chapter on the field of artificial intelligence will explore this question.

4 ARTIFICIAL INTELLIGENCE

Suppose you're sitting at a desk in a closed room. From time to time a conveyor belt delivers cards with Chinese characters written on them to your desk. You don't know how to read Chinese. But you must take the cards and process them according to a list of rules that you must follow exactly. When you finish with each group of cards, you place it on a conveyor belt that takes it out of the room. Outside the room is the person who has sent the cards into the room and who receives them when you are done.

Before you processed them, the cards didn't make sense to the person outside. After you processed them, they do. Your processing provided just as much information as if you were fluent in Chinese, that is, as if you had read the cards and made sense out of them all by yourself. In fact, the person waiting outside the room can't tell the difference. Did you perform an intelligent act?

In the "Chinese room" a human has worked with the cards in the same way a computer works with data. People who believe that the person was acting intelligently in the "Chinese room" may also believe that a computer can act intelligently—that it can think.

In the past, the question "can machines think?" could be answered "yes" only in science fiction, or like Moxon's chess player. Or the "yes" could be wishful thinking, as the people who watched The Turk may have done.

Today, the same question is being seriously asked and answered by computer scientists. Some say "yes"; others say "no." But this serious discussion is the foundation of a branch of science called artificial intelligence—AI, for short. And an intelligent computer could be the basis of an intelligent robot.

Artificial intelligence grew out of the development of the computer in the 1940s. It was in 1950 that Alan Turing, one of the founders of AI, stated the basic test of an intelligent computer:

If a computer can solve a problem that requires thought, and if a human expert cannot tell whether a computer or a human being solved the problem, then the computer was thinking when it solved the problem.

This "Turing test" is based on a simple idea, that thought is just moving symbols around, putting them together, and taking them apart. The idea can be stated the other way too: Moving symbols around is thought. That means the brain is a computer and nothing more. The idea is called *strong AI*, and it has many supporters. But it also has critics.

Other scientists believe that thought is more than combining, dividing, and rearranging symbols. They say that the Turing test is incomplete because thought includes understanding of the meaning of the symbols. They say that the "Chinese room" shows that processing symbols is not the same as intelligent thought.

A third group of scientists says that not enough is known about how humans think even to try building computers to do the same thing.

What Does the Human Brain Do?

If the human brain is a computer, it is a far more complex one than any built in a factory or laboratory. Combining and rearranging symbols is just part of the brain's work. It also has a way of storing information so that even the smallest clue of language or image can bring a whole idea, story, picture, or series of events into the person's mind. This is called *associative memory*.

It can use new knowledge to give meaning to something the person didn't understand before—the proverbial light bulb turning on or the "aha." The brain solves problems. It sets goals. And even in an uncertain or unexpected situation, it usually plans an action to get the person through it.

Intelligence

What does it mean to be intelligent? We humans define intelligence in terms of ourselves, so it is possible to define the term by seeing how a person works in the world. A normal person can understand the structure of living things, objects, and events—the way they are put together. A person understands how they relate to each other, and to him- or herself. A person knows how to change or rearrange them to make new relationships or even new things—to give them new meaning. Any person can make a plan to solve a problem, then carry it out, adjusting it along the way, if necessary. The same person can remember all this experience and knowledge, communicate it to others, and learn from it.

Each normal person is aware. The individual recognizes himself or herself and understands how everything else is "not self." A person knows what he or she knows and (usually) doesn't know, and how to act in each case.

Some of these skills are built into the human brain. Others must be learned. For instance, using a language to communicate seems to be built into the human brain. But people learn to speak English, Spanish, or another language.

There are different types and levels of intelligence. Some species are more "intelligent" than others, in terms of controlling and using their environment. For instance, orangutans are skilled at making and using tools; dogs and cats are not.

Artificial intelligence means computer intelligence. There are two ways to develop AI: Program a computer to act like the brain or program it to provide intelligent results, even if the method used to get them isn't brainlike.

Mind and Memory

Are a person's mind and memory the same as the brain? Mind and memory are very old ideas. They date back to the ancient Greeks, long before scientists began learning how the brain works.

The brain is a complex structure of cells (*neurons*), pathways, and electrical and chemical signals. They work together to process and store information. Today many scientists believe that the term *mind* means how the brain works, and *memory* is how it stores information. Memories are formed and kept in many parts of the *cortex*, the "smart" part of the brain. They are coordinated by another brain part called the *hippocampus*. But mind and memory are handy words, and even scientists continue to use them.

Learning

Memory is the storage of past problems that were solved, facts learned, sensory information, and emotions felt. Once someone learns how to ride a bicycle—balance on the two wheels, steer, lean into a curve—the brain retains the knowledge. People usually learn all these skills a few at a time. At each session, the brain stores what a person has learned. This means that next time the person can start where he or she left off, without starting again from the beginning. The skill might be self-taught or learned from a teacher or demonstrator.

Furthermore, the brain doesn't store bike-riding or other knowledge all by itself. A person can apply the knowledge learned about bike riding to other situations, such as riding a motor scooter or a motorcycle. It helps even when learning to drive a car. This type of learning is called *generalization*.

A computer or a robot is intelligent if it can learn things, follow examples or instruction, and develop its own method of learning how to solve a problem. It must be able to "remember" (store) this new knowledge in a way that it can use in the future. Many AI researchers are trying to develop systems that can generalize from their experiences and stored knowledge.

Are There Intelligent Artificial Systems?

Does anything called artificial intelligence actually exist? So far, the results have been mixed. But there have been some successes, mainly in what are called *expert systems*.

Expert Systems

Almost everyone at some time has gone to the doctor after feeling unwell, such as having an abdominal pain. In the examining room, the doctor usually asks the patient a series of questions, like: Where does it hurt? Have you been exercising? Did you eat anything unusual? The doctor or nurse probably takes the patient's temperature and pulse and listens to the heart and lungs with a stethoscope. After a few more questions, and some pressing on the abdomen, the doctor may decide to take a blood sample for testing. Once she has all the information, she compares it with what she learned in medical school and in her years of practicing medicine. She then rules out all but one possibility. Her diagnosis: a pulled muscle from playing volleyball. The patient will feel fine in a few days.

How did the doctor make the diagnosis? First of all, she needed knowledge of many different diseases and their symptoms. By asking questions, she learned about what the patient had done and eaten. She learned more about the person from the physical examination and the laboratory test. Once she had enough information, she used a series of rules to eliminate the most unlikely problems.

For instance, if the patient did not have a pain in the lower right abdomen and if the white blood cell count was not high, then she could decide that the patient probably didn't have appendicitis. If the temperature, breathing, and heartbeat were normal, she could decide to rule out other problems.

Expert systems or *knowledge-based systems* are computer programs that follow the same plan. Each one contains

- a body of knowledge,
- a method of getting information about a specific problem to be solved,
- a set of rules or another method to make use of the information, and
- a set of instructions for making decisions that solve the problem.

Why would anyone want an expert system to do what people are already so good at? The doctor in the example did just fine without a computer. But there are many situations where a physician can use help. For instance, a patient may have several medical problems that require treatment at the same time. Will medication for one problem interfere with the medication needed for another? What was the outcome for other patients in the same situation? Which combination of medicines works best? How have other doctors handled the situation? Are there two possible treatments? Which one would be better for this patient?

A doctor could put the basic information into an expert system. Then the computer could rule out unlikely diagnoses and treatments that probably won't work. This would let the doctor spend more time finding out about this particular patient and the best way to treat his illnesses.

Building an Expert System

Medicine is just one field where expert systems can be used. One can construct an expert system that contains the skills of business, technology, or of everyday life. An example from everyday life is the expertise needed to wash a car, perhaps to pass on the knowledge to someone who has no experience.

The first step is to define the subject and purpose of the system. The next step is to find a *domain* (area) expert, learn how he/she works, and put the expertise and method into the computer. The next step is to devise a method of reasoning.

The system also requires a program structure that holds the knowledge and reasoning method and lets the user pull out specific information and combine parts of it in different ways. The last element of the system is an *interface*, a way for someone else to use the computer and the expert system by asking for information or answers in plain English.

Domain Expert

An expert in a specific area has two types of knowledge. One type is the information itself. The other type is the method or way of using the information.

An expert at hand-washing, or detailing, a car knows the specific equipment needed: a bucket of water, a sponge, some detergent, a hose, and a drying cloth. Another part of the expertise is the method of washing the car, perhaps starting with the top and working downward, saving the trim and glass for last. An expert may have a unique way of using tools, for instance, a way of holding the hose to remove dirt from the tire wells. But that's just general skill. An expert also knows how to deal with unusual problems, such as removing road tar, achieving a brilliant shine without harming the paint, touching up scratches, and removing or concealing rust spots.

The point is, a general or quick description of accomplishing a goal isn't enough. The expert system must include the operations an expert may perform automatically, without even thinking about them. It may take careful questioning to learn some of the expert's methods. The system must also include adaptations of the expert's methods for unexpected conditions, such as how to wash a convertible.

Reasoning

Reasoning is the application of knowledge to present conditions and future plans. There are two major kinds of reasoning. One kind takes past experience and makes easy-to-use logical or practical rules from it. This is called *shallow* or *heuristic reasoning*. The other kind analyzes knowledge, experience, or a problem to find out its basic structure—what is called *deep reasoning*. Both kinds are used in expert systems.

Shallow or Heuristic Reasoning

Biologists and neuroscientists (scientists who study the brain and other parts of the nervous system) say that under stress, the body and brain are designed to help the person survive for approximately the next half-hour. Survival skills include quick thinking, improvising, using a plan that worked on an earlier occasion, using common sense, and even acting first, thinking later.

Everyone knows these strategies. People frequently use them while taking a test, on the athletic field, at a party, or in a frightening situation.

Sometimes heuristic or shallow reasoning is put in the form of rules like this one, often used by baseball batters at the plate: "If the last pitch was a slow one, then this pitch will be a fastball." A person can use these IF-THEN rules two ways for problem solving. One can work through a series of connected rules (a chain) until one reaches a conclusion or solves the problem— what is called *forward chaining*. Or the person can form a possible answer (a *hypothesis*) and work backward through the series of rules to see if they and the facts support it (*backward chaining*).

People may want to use both methods to solve a problem. One can work forward through the rules until it is possible to say "maybe the answer is so-and-so." Then the person works back from the end to see if the facts support the answer. For example, after a few questions in the examining room, the doctor probably decided that "a pulled abdominal muscle" was a good possible diagnosis for the patient's situation. Then the doctor worked backward through a series of IF-THEN rules to see if the blood test and abdomen examination supported the diagnosis.

Most of the expert systems now in use employ heuristic reasoning. They are sometimes called *first generation expert systems*. Medical diagnosis and treatment is very complicated, so several expert systems have been developed for medical use. One is Stanford University's ONCOCIN, which gives advice on how to manage cancer therapy. (The study of cancer is called oncology.) ONCOCIN asks for test results and other information about the patient. Then it takes its knowledge about the disease and various treatments, plus a large set of rules, and develops a plan for the patient's treatment. It can also revise the plan as treatment progresses and new information is entered.

CADUSEUS is another medical expert system, developed at the University of Pittsburgh. (It is named for the traditional symbol of medicine, showing wings and snakes wrapped around a staff.) It forms hypotheses based on over 100,000 cause-and-effect rules, then tests them against known causes and effects of several hundred diseases and symptoms.

Medicine isn't the only use for expert systems. Several are available to assist geologists looking for the best place to drill for oil. The searcher can enter information about a location's soil, underground formations, and other features into an expert system. It will respond by estimating with how likely an oil strike is. Other expert systems are used in business, particularly in evaluating credit applications.

The military uses expert systems too. Those for combat situations are called *battle management.* An expert battle manager plans a military action and oversees the movement of troops, weapons, and other equipment. The manager also knows how ready the troops are for battle and manages strategy and even the firing of weapons. It receives information as a battle progresses, so that it can update all its plans and make changes to meet new conditions. One in use by the U.S. Navy since the late 1980s is called FRESH (**F**orce **R**equirements **E**xpert **S**ystem).

Deep Reasoning

In real life, someone who has used heuristic reasoning to get through a tough situation may go back over it in his or her mind. This will allow the person to figure out what worked and what did not. The person may compare the situation to previous ones and see what they had in common. Such comparison may let the person determine how the situation might have been better handled. It may also provide expertise for successfully dealing with similar situations in the future.

This is deep reasoning. With it one analyzes a problem's structure, how it works, and how its parts interact. One uses the analysis to make a model solution for the problem. The model can also be adapted to handle other problems. Expert systems using deep reasoning are now under development. They are sometimes called *second generation expert systems.*

An example is ABEL, a medical system developed at MIT. It uses shallow reasoning to connect test and examination results with diseases. But it also uses deep reasoning to create models that show how diseases cause the symptoms that people have.

Deep reasoning is more thorough than shallow reasoning, but it takes time. This means that it does not work well in fast-changing situations that must use lots of information, like robotics.

The Future of Expert Systems

Scientists have been working on expert systems for several decades. They have learned that "being an expert" is much more complicated than they first thought. An effective expert system must have appropriate structures and rules. The computer's power, speed, and memory size are important too. Also, everyday knowledge and common sense are much more important than scientists first thought.

Two expert systems being developed in the 1990s are trying to overcome these problems. An expert system called Cyc will know 100,000,000 facts. It will have rules for mathematical facts as well as uncertainties and the current beliefs about them. And the developers hope its program will be able to use all this knowledge to solve real-life problems.

SOAR is another not-yet-finished system that is meant to include language, reasoning, memory, and emotion in its problem solving system.

Uncertainty

One of the main differences between the way a human thinks and the way a computer works is the kinds of questions to be dealt with. By design, today's computers handle YES-NO or TRUE-FALSE questions, like "2 + 3 = 6. True or false?" Many situations can be put in this format, and rules can be written to handle them.

Real life doesn't always work this way. Students, for example, often deal with questions like these: Is it going to snow today? Is my hair too long? Will I be able to get my homework done and still have time to watch television? In other words, many real life decisions involve questions where the answer is "some" or "maybe," instead of "yes" or "no." The word that covers such situations is *uncertainty*.

There are two kinds of uncertainty. Some things are not exact or precise, for instance, a sweater might be sort of red in color and slightly baggy. The other type of uncertainty involves the *chance* or *probability* that something will happen, or the degree to which something will happen. People deal with both kinds of uncertainty every day.

For instance, the morning weather report states that the day will be cloudy, with a 40 percent chance of snow. The view from the window shows a single fluffy white cloud in a blue sky. The question becomes what kind of clothes to wear. Does the person believe the weather forecast or think it's wrong? Perhaps the snow-laden clouds are just beyond the horizon.

Now suppose that the sky *does* show gray clouds, and the forecast is 40 percent chance of snow. This is less than a 50-50 chance. Again, does the person believe the forecast and what type of clothing is appropriate?

The person's decision will be based on several things. One factor is his or her past experience. Another is the opinion of a trusted family member. Personal choice in clothing is still another factor. People make decisions in a very uncertain situation like this all the time. A computer cannot do it even once.

Some expert systems have been equipped to handle a degree of uncertainty. Some do it with rules. Others use *certainty factors*, which give a different weight or importance to different kinds of fact and information. Sometimes the weight is how strongly the expert believes that the fact or information is true. For instance, the person in the previous example may believe that heavy, dark clouds in the morning always mean snow by afternoon. So that belief could be twice as important to the decision maker as the weather forecaster's statement that the clouds will be blown out of the area by midmorning.

Of course, we can always update our decision making if we get later or better information. For instance, if a gray sky starts turning blue before the person leaves the house, he or she may put the heavy boots back in the closet. Scientists call this process *nonmonotonic reasoning*. As with TRUE-FALSE reasoning, the object is to work with what one believes is true. The person then uses that belief to solve the problem.

Talking to Intelligent Systems

The most intelligent system in the world is valueless if people have trouble using it. The best way is to use English or some other human, or *natural*, language, rather than a computer language. That way the user and the computer can ask questions or display information as easily as two people talking on the phone or face to face.

Language is the main ability that separates humans from all other species. In fact, research is showing that the ability is built into our brains. We use language to communicate facts, ideas, stories, and emotions. Communicating with another person is hard enough. Even though we've all been using language since we were two years old, we still have problems. For instance, "Did you make your bed?" has a very different meaning than "You did make your bed, didn't you?"

To understand language, one must understand its structure (*syntax*) and its meaning (*semantics*). In addition to this basic understanding, one must be able to summarize what he or she reads or hears, or take a short statement and expand it. A person must be able to turn a statement into a question, or use one word in place of another.

A computer program that uses natural language will need those abilities too, though using a natural language with a computer is much harder than with another person. Once one begins talking to another person, words or thoughts can be left out, usually without destroying the meaning. People will expect an intelligent computer program to do the same thing. *Natural language processing* is a field of computer research that is showing slow but steady progress. The results are showing up in some expert systems and other areas of AI and robotics research.

Computers for AI

The computers people use have slowed the development of intelligent systems. Even most supercomputers—those that handle large amounts of data very fast—process problems one at a time, that is, *serially* or *sequentially*. This is the same way the first computers worked almost a half-century ago. AI needs more brainlike computers. Two of the most important new kinds of computer are parallel processors and neural networks.

Parallel Processing

Suppose a computer could work on several problems at the same time, or break a big or complex problem into sections and work on all of them at the same time. This *parallel processing* would be faster and more efficient for many problems. In fact, it would be much more brainlike.

The use of thousands of parallel processors to solve very large and very complex problems is called *massively parallel processing*. It will be needed for advanced robotics and for other intelligent problems. One massively parallel computer now in use is the Connection Machine, from Thinking Machines Corp. It uses 64,000 processors working together.

More efficient computer chips will let parallel processing computers be more powerful. In the future, massively parallel computers may use laser beams or other photons (particles of light), instead of electrical circuits. These *optical computers* could be 1,000 times as fast as today's computers and perform millions of parallel operations.

AI also needs computer languages that can handle brainlike computing.

AI Languages

The computer languages that most people use aren't designed to handle most complex AI problems. Widely used languages like

BASIC, PASCAL, FORTRAN, and C were designed to process numbers. But AI systems need to handle the English language, rules, and other idea structures. Two languages that are often used for AI are Lisp and Prolog.

Lisp (meaning **LIS**t **P**rocessing) processes lists of words, groups of words, and other lists, which can be flexibly rearranged or changed. For instance, each of the following names is a list:

(Susan)

(Michael)

(Bettina)

(David)

Each of these is a list that includes the original name and that person's brothers and sisters:

(Susan (Marcia))

(Michael ())

(Bettina (Andrew,William,John))

(David (Nicholas))

One could search the lists for people with no brothers or sisters. If Susan and David get married, one could add definitions that would let a person ask about the relationship of Marcia and Nicholas.

Prolog means **PRO**gramming in **LOG**ic. It is used to write series of rules that are backward chained to prove propositions. It is used in several different fields. Some AI developers like it because it can handle uncertainty. Suppose this database is in the computer:

birthday (anne,feb).

birthday (mark,apr).

birthday (kate,july).

birthday (paul,mar).

as in: Anne's birthday is in February.

One could then ask the computer questions, such as

?- birthday (anne,mar).

meaning "is Anne's birthday in March?" The computer would answer

no

If one asks

?- birthday (anne,x).

meaning "When is Anne's birthday?" the computer responds

x=feb

And the question

?- birthday (x,feb).

meaning "Who has a birthday in February?" is answered

x=anne

Brainlike Computers—Neural Networks

Massively parallel processing will be a great step toward brainlike computing. But an even greater step is now under way —the *artificial neural network*.

The brain's basic operating unit is a specialized cell called a neuron. Neurons are connected in networks, much like telephone networks. Neurons send signals that combine electricity and chemicals along fibers called *axons* and receive signals along other fibers called *dendrites*. A signal is transferred from axon to dendrite at a point called a *synapse*. Neurons don't work alone. They are organized in various levels of operation.

Problem solving takes place within a level and also between levels. A problem is usually divided up and given to different teams of neurons in different parts of the brain—what is called *parallel distributed processing*.

The artificial neural network—usually called simply a *neural network* or *neural net*—is loosely based on the brain model. This is partly because scientists have not discovered exactly how the brain works. An artificial neural network is composed of paths and nodes (sometimes called neurons).

The shortcuts that people often take to walk across a field or park help explain how a neural network works. Often, a person starts by trying several alternate shortcut routes before deciding on a regular one—the fastest or easiest route to the destination. Once the best basic path is selected, the person uses it regularly. At first, the path may be faint, but each time it is used, it becomes a little more distinct. Perhaps other people start using it, too, and soon all the grass is worn away. The best path, the one that gives the best results, becomes the most popular one.

Neural networks are good at pattern recognition, such as recognizing letters and numbers. Neural network computers that can recognize handwriting are being developed. Some experimental robots also use neural networks.

A network may have a single level or several. Each level contains many neurons or *nodes* on each level. If the network is given a number to identify, signals are first sent along all possible pathways between nodes. When processing is done, some of the paths lead to better answers than others do. They have done better at recognizing the number.

Then network training or learning begins. In the park story, the best path might be strengthened by being blacktopped. In a neural network, the pathways that lead to better answers are strengthened, so they will send more signals in the future. Paths that lead to incorrect answers are weakened, so they send few or no signals. When the network is fully trained, only the pathways that lead to correct answers—correctly recognizing the number—are carrying signals. The next time that number is put into the network, the strengthened pathway will recognize it quickly.

Scientists are constantly learning new things about how the brain works. What does all the new information mean for robotics? The next chapter will explore intelligence in advanced robots.

5 INTELLIGENT AND ADVANCED ROBOTS

Robotics and AI are closely connected. For many years, research-ers have wanted to use advanced, intelligent robotics as a special way to reach goals or solve problems. It is special for two reasons. First, robotics means physical action. A computer stays in one place and solves problems by manipulating electricity. A robot moves itself and other things. Second, people like their computers to work as fast as possible, but they do not usually put time limits on them. A robot's problem-solving and actions must take place in "*real time*"—time that is measured on the clock or in our own bodies. A person at bat in a softball game sees the ball coming and hits it in real time.

Does intelligent robotics mean a robot that can take a person's place in the "Chinese room" or pass the Turing test? Some people say it does. If so, are there any intelligent robots?

Are There Intelligent Robots?

The first robot meant to be intelligent was Shakey, built in the late 1960s at the Stanford Research Institute. Shakey was controlled by a large computer that communicated with it by radio. Shakey could see. It could navigate through its world using dead reckoning. It under-stood English language commands. It made plans and learned from experience. But Shakey worked in a very controlled and simplified world, not the everyday one. Even so, Shakey couldn't make quick decisions.

Since then, improvements have been slow. There are no truly intelligent robots yet. That is partly because there are no truly intelli-gent computers.

Shakey was built in the late 1960s by Stanford Research Institute.

[With permission of SRI International]

Better bodies are also required for intelligent robots. They will need more humanlike hands and better ways to move around. Teleoperation and sensors must be improved. And they will have to transmit more realistic information to their human operators or overseers—what is called *telepresence*.

How Smart Should Robots Be?

How smart a robot is depends on how one defines intelligence. In the 1990s, there are several ways to define robotic "intelligence." One definition follows AI research. Other scientists are defining intelligence more in terms of sensors—how much of the world the robot detects and how the controller uses the information. Still other scientists are examining a robot's behavior as it interacts with its world, rather than in terms of its brain power.

Artificially Intelligent Robots

According to AI research, before a robot can do any intelligent work, its brain needs the basic AI skills: expert knowledge and decision-making power, ready for use. The kinds of work robots are being designed to do may be surprising. Some jobs may seem simple, for instance, reading the utility meters in people's houses—the meters that measure how much gas, electricity, or water is used. To read the meter someone just has to look at the dials and write down the numbers, or draw lines on a diagram showing where the dial arrows or needles are pointing.

Being able to read the meter is one of the important intelligent skills of an advanced robot named Hermies, built at Oak Ridge National Laboratory. Hermies, actually a series of robots with that name, has several "advanced" features. It has two arms, one with 7 DOF. It can navigate through its environment. And it has advanced sensors. It also has more computer power than most robots. It carries a parallel computer with 16 processors that lets the robot move autonomously to its work place. It can then quickly perform a complex task. It has

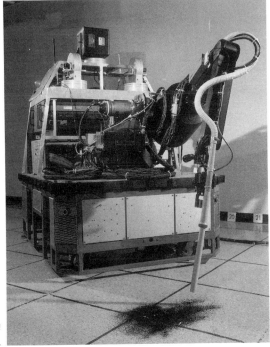

(Oak Ridge National Laboratory Photo)

Hermies III, a 2,700-pound mobile robot developed and built at Oak Ridge National Laboratory, uses a vacuum hose attached to its manipulator arm to remove a deliberate spill. The exercise was part of a test of the robot's ability to make its own decisions on how to complete the task.

69

additional computer power in a separate controller. The parallel computer has an expert system for navigation, with rules for decision making.

Isn't it a little silly to use all this computing power to read a utility meter? Not at all. Reading the meter involves planning, sensor analysis, and complex control—all intelligent actions. First the robot must see the meter and get close enough to read it. It has to navigate carefully and park straight in front of the meter, so its reading will be accurate. Then its vision processor locates the needles, which it registers as lines. Next it computes the needle angle on the dial. Finally it finds the angle on a table in its program that gives the correct reading.

An intelligent robot needs a plan to follow as it works. The plan should include goals along the way. It should also be able to deal with failures and—most of all—the unexpected. The robot also has to learn from its experiences. And it has to be aware of what it knows and doesn't know.

Planning

People make plans for their own actions all the time. Planning involves a person setting down each action that must be taken to achieve a goal. One must know the amount of time each action requires. One also must decide the order in which each action is to be started and at what point in the plan each must be finished.

One must also figure out whether actions will overlap. For instance, in the car-washing sequence, a wax may need time to dry before a person can begin polishing. The waiting time can be used as a rest period, or it can be used on other washing activities, such as cleaning the hubcaps, wiping the windows, or vacuuming the inside. By the time those chores are done, the person can return to polishing.

Robotic planning can take several forms. The controller can store a series of general plans, then adapt the one most suited to a specific situation. In another example, a person may know how to paint large surfaces with a roller and paint tray, and how to use a brush to paint small areas. Each one is a general plan. One can customize the roller-and-tray plan for specific projects, like painting a room wall.

The controller can also take an old plan that worked well and adapt it. Suppose a sentry robot patrols the hallways of a company's building. When the company moves to a new building, one can adapt the robot's old operating plan to the new geography.

Another type of planning is the one people use in real life, for instance, when the toast burns during breakfast preparation, or when a barricaded road forces people to take an alternative route. In these cases, a person starts with a plan, but changes it as the action proceeds and conditions change, or if the plan isn't working well. A robot's plan can use the same method.

Planning has another side, too. Sometimes it includes understanding someone else's plan from his or her actions. Opponents in individual or team sports do this frequently. Diplomats, business executives, and generals must try to predict the other side's strategy and tactics. Then they can adapt their own plans or make new ones.

One way to analyze someone's action is by breaking it into its basic parts. This is like taking a machine apart to see how the pieces fit together. Another way is to try to understand why the actions are taking place—what purpose they serve. Then one can predict actions that will also serve that purpose. Or one can write an IF-THEN rule: IF the light in room 128 is on at night, THEN it's all right for people to be moving around the area. Therefore, the sentry robot will not send an alarm signal.

Knowing the order in which events take place is very important in planning. Does the robot's arm begin moving toward the assembly line before the part arrives, after it arrives, or just as it arrives?

Planning for Automated Factories

Planning skills will be very important in the future when robots work with other planned and programmed systems in totally automated factories. Computers and robots will perform all the operations, including ordering materials, producing parts, assembling them, and preparing them for shipment.

Assembly and other operations will be coordinated with the help of an AI *planner*. This is an intelligent computer system that sets goals and priorities. It takes into account the product wanted, the numbers to be produced, and the type of equipment and materials needed. It definitely includes the way assembly robots interact with their work environment. Robots with several arms will be at work. Teams of robots will work together. Many operations will be going on at the same time. Each will have its own plan, but all the plans will have to work together, too.

AI Planning for Buying Robots

How does one shop for an industrial robot? Most companies do it by comparing features on various models, talking to salespeople, and observing what models other companies are buying and using. It's the same process an individual uses to buy a bicycle or an automobile. Like any piece of equipment, a robot is expensive. The buyer wants to be sure it will do its work and fit into the overall manufacturing plan. The decision will be even harder to make for advanced, intelligent robots. Where can companies turn for help?

Soon it will be possible to use AI. Scientists in Germany, Czechoslovakia, and elsewhere are experimenting with expert systems that decide which robot is best for the buyer's needs.

Using AI this way expands the idea of AI planning for factory production. A German expert system starts by asking the purchaser: Do you really need robots for the tasks you want done? If so, what characteristics do you want for your robot?

The expert system also helps the purchaser choose among the hundreds of models for sale by comparing each model's features with the tasks he or she wants done. To answer these questions, the system builds the knowledge base. The German system contains 200 plans for using robots in various ways. It also holds all the specifications of the robots on the market. And it analyzes 500 automated tasks.

The specific information that the expert system needs about the buyer's factory is also entered, such as the tasks to be done and kinds of material to be worked on. For instance, a question on the screen asks: Which motion system do you want? (choose one)

electrical
pneumatic
hydraulic

The system also asks questions about the type of grippers needed and what tasks will be performed. The buyer can also draw a diagram of the robot's work area showing its size, layout, where the robot will be placed, and what other equipment will be there.

Now the system goes to work by comparing each task, material, and other job characteristic with every robot on the market. Each variation is a robotic world. The worlds are compared to the one the buyer has created. If no robot is exactly right for the buyer, the system makes tradeoffs among robot features. Finally, it comes up with the "best buy," and it explains its decision.

Another expert system, by Czechoslovakian scientists, helps design a robotic assembly line. The program is written in the AI language Prolog. It forms rules from information about available robots and the tasks to be done. Then it uses the rules to make its choice.

Most planning for intelligent robotics will be about the robot's tasks. Then the plans must be transferred into arm and hand motions. This is an advanced form of teaching and learning.

Intelligent Teaching and Learning

How does one teach a robot to give a sheep a haircut? It's hard enough to teach a robot to do assembly line work. Teaching one to work in the outside world is even more complicated. Shearing a sheep is like giving the animal a skinhead haircut, only all over its body. A human shearer has to hang onto a squirming animal, then use electric clippers to quickly take off all the wool, without injuring either of them in the process. Doing the job well requires great skill.

Some Australian robotics scientists took on the job of teaching a robot to shear a sheep this way. First, they used computer graphics to design a generic 3-D sheep. Then they gave it the measurements and shape of a specific animal. They added the shape changes caused by breathing and other natural sheep movements. An expert sheep shearer's hand and body movements were added in. When everything worked on the computer, the scientists programmed the shearing motions into a robotic arm and clipper hand. It took the scientists several years to put the whole system together.

Introspection

The final AI skill an intelligent robot needs is *introspection*, the ability to examine its own reasoning methods. This lets the robot tell the difference between what it knows and what it doesn't know. Introspection will let an autonomous robot react faster and better in a changing environment, enabling it to decide whether to act on its best knowledge or wait until it has more or better information.

Better Robot Bodies

Every robotics scientist and engineer would like to have fully autonomous robots at work in the real world. But that's for the future. Right now, robots are showing increased intelligence by their use of advanced teleoperation and sensing, and by putting their human operators on the scene with a "you are there" technique called telepresence.

(UPI/Bettmann News Photos)

When this photo was taken in 1987, this robot hand was the most advanced, most humanlike hand ever developed. It was the product of a collaboration between the University of Utah and MIT. The robot hand is shown here with the human hand of MIT associate professor of brain and cognitive science John Hollerbach.

For robots, better intelligence requires better bodies. This includes improved hands. The hands (end effectors) should be *dexterous*. That is, they should have several jointed fingers and an opposable thumb—the outstanding feature of the human fingers and one that makes humans distinct from the great apes. Flexible cables serve as tendons to bend and straighten the fingers.

Mobility must be improved too. Robotic wheelchairs, forklifts, and carts are all being tested with new types of wheels. They can move, turn, and go over obstacles at the same time. The purpose is to improve dead reckoning navigation over rough surfaces. For instance, if the wheels can roll over an obstacle instead of going around it, there's less chance of getting lost.

Some walking robots have been equipped with touch sensors on their legs. They work like insects' feelers. They can reach out and touch the ground or stairs to know where to step next.

Advanced Teleoperation

Teleoperated remote vehicles and programmed robots are being employed for specific tasks. Future systems must put the two technologies together. This way, they will make better use of human operators, expert systems, and intelligent machines.

This will involve:

- Real-time expert systems to control on-line robots as they perform their tasks in, for example, hazardous environments.
- Improved vision and force sensing, so that the controller can use the sensors' information for making decisions while a task is in progress.
- Force-reflecting servomanipulators that are more reliable and easier to keep working accurately and reliably.

Another way of defining a robot's intelligence is how much of the environment its sensors detect.

Advanced Sensing

Walking down a familiar hallway is a highly predictable process, requiring routine skills. People usually don't notice where they are, except to keep from bumping into someone. Today's sentry robots are skilled enough for patrolling predictable areas. But the detection skills they provide are not thorough enough for many situations where the highly unusual can occur: military posts, "high-tech" industrial plants, or other high-security areas. An intelligent system also verifies the findings and assesses the situation.

High security robots need intelligent skills. One such skill is environmental awareness, interpreting many signals provided by humanlike sensors. Another is good navigation, the ability to move accurately through the building. The third is making fast and correct decisions.

Robart II, an advanced mobile sentry robot developed by Cmdr. H. R. Everett at the Naval Ocean Systems Center, shows how a controller can take information from many sensors and use it to move intelligently in the real world.

Brain

Robart's intelligence comes from 13 computers in the robot's body that control its actions and take in "real time" sensory information.

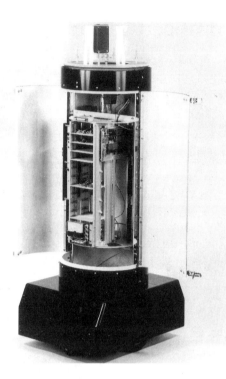

Robart II, an autonomous sentry robot developed by the U.S. Navy

(Official U.S. Navy photograph)

The computers also monitor the robot's own operation and report abnormalities to the controller.

An ordinary personal computer performs the intellectual work as controller. This means planning navigation routes, keeping the two-dimensional "world" map up to date, and telling Robart how to avoid obstacles. With this system, the robot moves through ordinary offices and hallways and avoids known obstacles. When it confronts unexpected chairs and wastebaskets, it plans new routes around them. When Robart returns to its starting place, it automatically avoids the new obstacles found on the outbound trip.

The controller computer also evaluates the security situation. Robart has several kinds of sensors, 128 in all. Some are designed to detect intruders or other security problems. Other sensors help Robart navigate.

Environmental Sensors

Robart's environmental sensors tell the controller whether building conditions are normal or not. They measure temperature, relative humidity, barometric pressure, light and noise levels, toxic gas, smoke, and fire.

The robot also takes its own temperature, to tell if the system is working normally.

Navigation System

Robart uses dead reckoning, its world map, and sensory information to navigate through its territory. A stereo vision system lets it see where it is going and compare the view with the map stored in the planner. Twenty-four range-finding sonar detectors circle Robart's swiveling "head." They help the robot keep track of its location as it travels.

Its bumpers contain touch sensors that tell which part of the bumper has collided with something. Each sensor is a tiny switch that sends a signal to the controller, which decides how to move past the obstacle. Infrared sensors located near Robart's wheels detect the floor. As long as it can "see" the floor, Robart won't fall down stairs or tip over crossing a dangerously high floor threshold.

This information goes to the brain, which tries to plan a new route. If it cannot, it uses voice synthesis to call for human help.

Intrusion Sensors

The environmental and navigational sensors and the navigation system let Robart perform its intelligent sentry duty. It has an whole different team of sensors to help: six different types of sensor detect human intruders and infrared (heat) sensors detect body heat. A moving person casts shadows and blocks light. This can be recorded by sensors that register differences in light level.

Ultrasound (sonar) can detect human motion inside a building just as it can a submarine's movement under water. Microwaves, similar to radio waves, also detect motion by changes in the wave's size and shape. These waves can go through walls, the way a radio's incoming waves do, and detect motion on the other side. A video camera detects motion by comparing a current picture of the scene with a picture of the way the scene should be, stored in the computer.

Other sensors monitor vibrations, which might be made by a moving person. A sound system picks up noises.

If there is a possible threat, having many sensors is important. The microwave motion detector might pick up something that the other motion detectors didn't. The robot's sound detector may have heard something at the same time, but the building alarms may or may not have gone off. The controller takes all the sensor information and compares it with information stored in its memory about "normal" and "alarm" conditions. Then it makes a decision.

These multiple sensors also make it harder for intruders to beat the system. It takes more time and skill to disable or fool several different kinds of sensor than a single one. Once Robart detects an intruder, it will follow it and speak a command to stop. Its video camera provides a picture of the situation to human security guards.

Telepresence

Ordinary tools are fine for some situations, but there's nothing like being on the scene and touching the object. The sensors and manipulators on today's tethered robots—such as undersea explorers—may give the operator considerable control over robot operations. This, as you have already learned, is called teleoperation. Telepresence transfers the robot's sensory experience to the operator.

Telepresence can show:

- **Position** People commonly reach far back into a dark but well-known closet for something on the floor. Even without looking, one can judge location. The touch of a clothes hanger may signal the person to reach farther back and down.
- **Texture and rigidity** Someone reaching for a tennis ball knows just what it should feel like: small, round, slightly rigid, and fuzzy. On touching a shoe or a volleyball, one knows instantly that it isn't the tennis ball.
- **Size and weight** People quickly learn to judge the weight and content of an object to be moved, as when carrying a trash can. By touching it and moving it just a bit, one can tell whether it's full and heavy, or only partly full and much lighter. This sensory information tells how much strength the person needs to pick it up and carry it.
- **Force and torque** When beginning to remove the cap from a jar, the feel of the cap, plus past experience, tells the person how much twisting motion (torque) to use.
- **Environmental conditions** Even without touching anything, one's hand (and other skin) sensors can feel heat and cold and wind.

For a telerobot to do these jobs, telepresence could let the human operator experience them just as vividly, even from very far away. The key elements of telepresence are sensors, manipulators, hands, and vision systems that are almost as good as human ones.

Equipment for Telepresence

What equipment does a robot need to provide telepresence? According to some experts, it should have at least two arms and hands that work together. The arms need 7 DOF with force control. They should be strong enough to lift, hold, and move large objects. The hands should be able to grasp things. They need force indicators and controllers. To see what the robot sees, the operator needs a head-mounted vision display. An experimental telepresence system developed for the U.S. Marine Corps includes a vision helmet.

Using Telepresence

What do you do with all this information? Most research is for use in the military and in space. Exploring the ocean floor and deep beneath the Earth's surface are other possibilities. All these environments are dangerous and uncertain.

Telepresence will be vital in unknown places where conditions can change at any moment. Suppose the robot is exploring underground geologic formations. This means many uncertainties for the human operator in deciding how to interact with the formations. If the robot lifts a particular rock, for example, will the surface cave in under it? So, the robot's sensory information should also be fed into a computer program that can predict what will happen after the operator acts. Based on the sensors' readings, the computer can simulate the operator's action. Then it can decide "it is safe to lift the rock and carry it ten feet away," or "if the robot picks up the rock, the ground will cave in under it."

Telepresence will also be used with autonomous robots. Even though they will be working on their own, they will send back real-time reports to human supervisors.

Some scientists have taken an even more sensor-oriented approach: They have developed robots that interact intelligently without any brains (controllers) at all.

Brainless, but Intelligent Robots

The purpose of robots has always been to do jobs that people ordinarily do, whether on the spot or remotely. They expand and extend our physical abilities. Intelligent robots use human skills as they work—planning, setting goals, and achieving them. But are plans, reasoning, and goals really the way people interact with the world? Or do we usually follow some well-established behavior patterns that let us sense the world, then react and interact with it as it changes? Suppose "intelligence" is the way we really interact with the world.

A familiar example of depending on the senses to understand our surroundings is a Halloween "haunted house." It is an environment meant to trick our senses and trigger fear, even though people know it is all in fun. The haunted house is mostly dark, so that the senses of touch and sound must do most of the work. Reaching for a wall and feeling a curtain or cobweb, or tripping over an unknown object, make it hard to form a mind-picture of what one is experiencing. Finally, by moving cautiously, and following other sensory clues, such as a breeze or a ray of light, one can successfully complete the trip through the "house." In other words, people use their intelligence by reacting to the environment and successfully moving through it.

Some robot scientists believe that these behavior patterns can be the basis for intelligent robots. One such scientist is Rodney Brooks at Massachusetts Institute of Technology, who has developed robots that work on the principle of behavior patterns. Genghis is one of his robots. Genghis is small, about 14 inches long. But like its "conqueror of the world" namesake Genghis Khan, it is powerful. When the six-legged robot walks around or climbs over a book, its behavior patterns are at work.

A robot like this doesn't start out "smart." Brooks's robots start simply, by sensing the environment and end by taking action. If the robot is moving and it senses an obstacle, it moves around it. When this behavior works well, a slightly more advanced behavior can be added.

Someone in a haunted house moves through it more intelligently as he or she senses things and reacts to them. The robots work in roughly the same way. If everything goes well with the robot's simpler types of behavior, layers of even more advanced behavior can be added. First Genghis stands up. When it accomplishes this, it can also walk. If it is successful, it can also start climbing over books and other obstacles. Eventually, Genghis, or one of its successors, will have even "smarter" behavior patterns. For instance, it will create a map of its world as it explores and use it to avoid running into things.

Genghis works without having a central controller. Instead, each behavior "layer" is controlled independently. But the layers communicate, so that no advanced behavior can start unless the simpler ones are up and running, just as one cannot start walking until one stands up.

Genghis's sensors tell it about its world as it moves on its six legs, each with 2 DOF. The sensors detect its pitch (motion up and down) and roll (as in rolling over, or perhaps falling sideways off a book). It also has heat and force sensors.

According to Brooks, studying a robot's behavior in the real world provides information one can't get from studying a more complex robot in a controlled world. He compares it to studying animal behavior in the wild, rather than in a laboratory setting.

Microrobots

As small as Genghis is, other working robots are even smaller—so small that they are invisible to the human eye. Some are only about one-fifth the size of the period at the end of this sentence.

Such *microrobots* are being developed for medical treatment. One works as a pump in an artificial pancreas to treat diabetes. A process called micromachining is producing tiny motors and sensors 100 micrometers (μm) in diameter that are made of silicon, the same material used to make computer chips.

Microrobots are actually close relatives of the computer chip. Microdevices are made in much the same way that computer chips are (though other techniques are also used, and other materials are also being studied). Computer chips are wafers of the element silicon on which integrated circuits are etched. The leading work in development is being done at the Massachusetts Institute of Technology and the University of California, Berkeley.

The process has been used to make pressure sensors so small that three can fit on the head of a pin. Microrobots are possible because the world of the very small is different from the world we know.

One such difference involves the direct conversion of electrical energy into mechanical energy, what is called the piezoelectric effect. This effect is too weak to be useful in normal-scale activities, including normal-sized robotic actions. But it can be extremely useful in the world of the very small. A six-legged microrobot uses it to move individual biological cells in a laboratory dish, making it a useful future tool for biomedical research and medical treatment.

Micromechanics studies the movement and behavior of tiny machines as small as 100 μm in diameter. Very small, lightweight devices behave differently—relate to their environment differently—than large, heavy ones do. For instance, an ant can carry a large piece of dirt. A bug can walk across the surface of a pond.

An ant has a tiny mass (the measure of its ability to accelerate when a force acts on it). So the forces of inertia (the tendency to stay in one place or to move in a straight line) and gravitation (attraction between masses) are much less than on an elephant or a person. Several scientists have pointed this out: If you reduce something's volume 100 times, you decrease its mass 1,000,000 times. Inertia and gravitation decrease by the same amount.

Some forces are more important for bodies with a smaller mass than they are for bodies with a large mass. Electrostatic attraction—the force that makes dust stick to a mirror—decreases only 10,000 times when volume is reduced 100 times. This makes electrostatic force much greater than gravitation—on objects with a small mass. Also, electromagnetic forces are much less on tiny objects than on large ones. This means that electrostatic forces are more important than electromagnetic forces. Another way large and small masses behave differently involves surface tension, which increases with the area of a surface. All of these physical laws are why a tiny bug can walk across the surface of a large body of water.

Friction and wear as parts rub against each other are different also, making microdevices the object of study of the discipline called *tribology* (in Greek, *tribos* means rubbing). This is important for several reasons. Scientists estimate that one-third of all the energy in the world goes to waste as friction. Friction cuts the efficiency of robots and other machines by reducing their output of useful energy, information, or communications signal. This is because when machine parts rub against each other, their physical and chemical properties change. They stretch, or become hot, or fail to work the way they're supposed to. Also, some of the material is worn off and thrown into the environment as waste and possibly pollution. Research is now underway to find out how friction and wear affect microrobots.

Some day, microrobots designed for the micro-world may be used routinely in intelligent valves and pumps implanted in the human body. They could help people with physical disabilities. They could even be sent to specific body locations, perhaps through genetic engineering techniques. Even microrobots may seem big, compared to the next generation. These are *nanorobots*, 1,000 times smaller.

Of all the places where advanced, intelligent robots will be used, outer space is one of the most exciting. The next chapter looks at the place of robots in space.

6 ROBOTS IN SPACE

Robots have long been part of the exploration of space. Astronauts on the Space Shuttle have used a teleoperated robotic arm to launch communications satellites into orbit. As long ago as 1977, the U.S.'s *Viking 1* and *2* landed robotic probes on Mars to analyze the soil and atmosphere. The U.S.S.R.'s *Venera 12* and *13* landed on Venus in 1978 and 1981. True to this tradition, even more skilled robots will play important roles in future space missions. These include a permanent U.S. station in space and, later, bases on the moon and Mars.

People have long dreamed of going to Mars. Besides the desire to explore the unknown, scientists already know that space outposts could provide mineral resources, energy, and even new homes for people.

In the United States, the program is called the Space Exploration Initiative. But the project is too big for any one nation. Too much research, design, and development is needed, and it will cost too much. The project is already a joint operation. It will probably include Russia (and perhaps other former Soviet republics), Japan, the European Community, and others.

Cost and the hazards of working and living in space are the two main reasons robotics will play a great role in this expanded space program. Robotics is most valuable in three types of situations: where human life could be endangered, where the use of humans is very expensive, and where repetitive tasks requiring great precision will be performed. Outer space provides all three of these conditions. Robots will be used for exploration, construction, and operation.

Are space robots different from earthbound ones? Earth's atmosphere protects us from extremes of heat, cold, and radiation. Working in space can be hazardous for machines as well as people. Weightlessness won't affect robots the way it does humans, but temperature and radiation will.

The space shuttle Challenger *on a February 1984 flight. The remote manipulator system is visible in the cargo bay.*

(NASA)

Space robots must be made of materials that can withstand temperatures ranging from 400° F in the sun to over 200° below zero in the shade. Electromagnetic radiation (gamma rays) can also damage both materials and electronic circuitry. Another hazard is damage from flying objects. These can be meteorites or pieces of space junk left over from previous missions.

Humans working in space must wear heavy suits to protect them from all these hazards. This slows down their work rate. Scientists have decided that it is better for well-designed robots to work under these hazardous conditions than people.

Robots on the U.S. Space Station

Some time during the 1990s, The U.S. National Aeronautics and Space Administration (NASA) plans to begin building an advanced

(NASA)

An artist's conception of Space Station Freedom shows the station in its completed, permanently staffed state.

orbiting space station for scientific and commercial research. Plans for Space Station Freedom, as it is called, include many robots to help assemble and service the station, as well as to perform research tasks. If automated manufacturing is performed, robots will take part.

The former U.S.S.R. has had a space station in orbit for many years. The station planned by the United States will be designed around flexible and intelligent systems. Humans, computers, and robots will work in teams. Space robots will need a combination of teleoperation and autonomous control. Robot arms and hands must be very flexible. Researchers are working on hands with 20 DOF. Robotic vision systems should be in color and 3-D. Other sensing systems must also be as close to human quality as possible because telepresence will be important for the human crew members. At some time in the future, scientists expect space robots to be almost completely autonomous.

As on Earth, the robots will work in hazardous environments and perform tasks too hazardous for people. Robots will also take on tasks that are too routine for highly trained, and expensive, astronauts and technical specialists to spend time on. A farming robot with a seed-

Eva Retriever, a human-sized robot, shown as she might later work, hovering in space. Eva was designed as part of a solution to the anticipated problem of accidental separation in space.

(NASA)

planting hand might even plant hydroponic gardens (grown without soil) and harvest crops for the space station's human crew. Finally, the robots will service and repair themselves.

The most dangerous and expensive human tasks will be those that take place outside the station. Robotics could reduce both the danger and the cost of what is called EVA (ExtraVehicular Activity).

Station Assembly

Assembly of the space station will be a space version of the assembly of an advanced automated factory on Earth. The Space Shuttle will bring parts up to orbit from Earth. Robots and humans would work as a team to assemble subsections, then put the entire station together. The beams (basic supports) could be assembled using a teleoperated robot with stereo vision, a very flexible hand with force and torque sensors, and two arms. An all-purpose arm would be paired with a second one specially designed to handle and rotate the very long beams.

Use on the Space Station

Space Station Freedom could be finished by 1999. When it goes into operation, robots will be at work all over it—on the inside, the outside, and even flying around it. Robots will load and unload materials and samples for scientific and manufacturing experiments. They will rearrange work areas. They will move materials between the station and the shuttles from Earth. And robots will fly from the station to service and repair satellites. Or they will fly around the station adjusting sensors or other equipment.

What space station robots look like will depend on what their jobs are. One that is expected to do a space version of skyscraper construction is the Flight Telerobotic Servicer (FTS).

The Flight Telerobotic Servicer

The Flight Telerobotic Servicer (FTS) is a robot that could be used to assemble the space station and later for maintenance, inspection, and servicing of outer, unpressurized areas. It looks almost like an astronaut in a space suit. The FTS has a body made of three segments connected by joints. It has two jointed arms with 7 DOF, as well as a single central "leg" that anchors at the worksite. Each of the arms has gripper end effectors that use tools that are stored in slots on the "abdomen." Its "head" contains a four-camera vision system—two wide angle cameras that are held out from the body, plus one camera on each wrist for close-ups of the end-effectors at work. The FTS is powered and controlled two ways. An umbilical cord attached to its back from a human-controlled workstation can provide power and data communications. Or it can use a battery pack and antennas.

The robot will be moved to its work site by the manipulators of a space station transportation system. The system's manipulators can also serve as telerobotic manipulators controlled by the operator. Or it can work detached.

Satellite Servicing

Robots that fly by themselves will be expected to handle much of the work of servicing and repairing satellites. In some cases, a robot may have a combination of teleoperated and autonomous control. For instance, the robot may be able to find and take hold of the satellite on its own. If it cannot, it can be teleoperated for part of the maneuver. For a task such as bolting two parts together, a human operator could teleoperate the robot to its work area. Then the robot would become autonomous, using its own programming and sensors to pick up tools. The operator once again would put it in the correct work position. Finally, the robot would autonomously perform its task. As technology develops totally autonomous robots, they will take over most of the satellite servicing and other tasks.

Robots for Exploring the Mars Surface

The purpose of any expedition to Mars is to learn as much as possible about the Red Planet—so-called because much of its sand-swept surface looks red from Earth. Since ancient times the planet has been named for various gods of war or death. The name Mars comes from the ancient Roman war god.

Mars has always fascinated people. It is one of the Earth's nearest neighbors—if something as much as 250 million miles away can be called "near." Its size is about half that of Earth; its mass, one-tenth that of our planet; and its density, three-fourths that of Earth. Mars

(NASA)

This full-scale model of the Viking lander, here shown against a Marscape, was on exhibit at 3rd Century America, the U.S. Bicentennial Exposition on Science and Technology in 1977.

takes about 23 Earth months to complete its elliptical orbit around the Sun. Each Martian "day"—a complete rotation on its axis—is called a *sol* and takes about 24½ hours. Because of Mars's smaller size, its gravity is much less than Earth's.

Flights to Mars began in 1962, with the former U.S.S.R.'s Mars 1, which was lost on the journey. Between 1965 and 1969, several U.S. and U.S.S.R. spacecraft flew by Mars or orbited the planet. The first soft landing on Mars was by the Soviet *Mars 3* spacecraft in 1971.

All the information we have from the planet's surface has been provided by the partly robotic American *Viking 1* and *2* landers. The Viking probes were controlled from Earth. The long distance meant that there were long delays before a command sent from Earth to move a rock, for instance, would be carried out. However, they sent back photographs and data during the 1970s and 1980s, informing us that surface conditions are very different on the two planets.

Mars is 1½ times as far from the Sun as Earth is, and its atmosphere—mostly carbon dioxide—is much thinner. This means that Mars gets much less heat from the Sun. Mars is a very cold, dry desert, with temperatures near -100° F (a little colder than Antarctica) and no surface water. The Mars atmosphere is mostly carbon dioxide, and its polar caps are a combination of ordinary (water) ice and dry ice (frozen carbon dioxide).

Mars is between 35 and 250 million miles from Earth, depending on where the two planets are in their orbits. The trip will be somewhere in between. A spaceship will need a spiraling course needed to get there. This is because the spacecraft must escape Earth's gravity and avoid the Sun and other planets. So the actual journey from Earth could be 100 million miles long.

Because of the physical conditions, plus the high cost of putting people into space, scientists plan to launch 20 automated ships, called probes, between 1999 and 2005. These ships will carry the next generation of space robots.

Mars Robots—the Next Generation

When each probe lands, it will release robots and other equipment. Some of the robots will be roving vehicles. Some are expected to be small behavioral robots, the descendants of Genghis and others like it. The equipment will collect information about weather, ground conditions, and possible earthquake activity and send it back to Earth or to an orbiting spacecraft.

The next Mars robots will have to work in uncertain conditions; cooperate; and cut, carry, and perhaps analyze interesting samples. The robots will have different abilities and intelligence. Some of them will be controlled by human operators, while others will work more independently but under human supervision. The robots will have to be able to move around their territory, accurately sense conditions, and make judgments as they carry out their tasks.

Scientists began developing the next generation of Mars robots shortly after Viking. These new robots will have many more abilities, including autonomy, based on technology developed since the early 1970s. An autonomous robot could use its vision system to analyze what it saw. Then it could plan its route and, with the help of range-finding, force, and touch sensors, rove the area on its own. It could then carry out tasks with no time delay.

Among the new-generation robots is a Micro-Rover that scientists at the Jet Propulsion Laboratory call Rocky. Rocky is a six-wheeled, flexible-bodied cart with camera, 3-DOF scoop to pick up samples, an antenna, and a sample collection box. The robot can move in a given direction for a specified distance. Autonomous abilities include avoiding and maneuvering around obstacles and hazards. It can also autonomously decide whether a location is suitable for soil collection. If it is, Rocky will collect the sample, then return to its starting place.

(NASA)

The Mars Rover Sample Return Mission, a candidate for launch in the late 1990s, is a joint undertaking involving JSC and NASA. This photo shows one of several design concepts being studied for a robotic Mars rover, which would collect rock samples from the planet's surface.

Other skills are being added. By the time it is launched, Rocky should be able to sense its environment, plan its actions, monitor its environment, carry out its assignments, and change its behavior to meet changing conditions.

Rocky is just one of the robots that will probably work on Mars. With improved technology, some of the robots could be maneuvered remotely, by scientists or astronauts using telerobotics and telepresence.

All the robots will have some AI abilities. They will have to keep track of their environment and their own operations. They'll have to make plans and carry them out and receive feedback on how the plans worked. If necessary, they may have to change or adapt the plans for the next set of goals. If there are errors in operations, the robots will have to find the cause. They will need to learn from past experience, in order to improve their performance. They will have to be able to tell the difference between what they know and don't know, so they won't try to perform tasks that they aren't qualified for. And they will have to give themselves the robotic version of first-aid, if needed.

The people who design the Mars robots have to be sure the robots are able to do complex tasks in the Martian environment. They must answer these questions: Will the remote systems be able to perform autonomously? Will they hold up under Martian conditions? How will tasks and abilities be divided among the various robots?

The degree of autonomy has not yet been determined. The robots will have to be capable of more than teleoperation (master-slave manipulation), mainly because of the distance from Earth to Mars. The master's signals would take too long to get to the robot, making "real-time" control impossible.

Fully autonomous robots would be very useful, and as you have seen, some are available now for simple tasks. But autonomous robots for complex tasks do not yet exist.

Robots operating under supervised autonomy from Earth or from orbiting spacecraft *are* possible. Humans will do the thinking and make the judgments. The robots would sense the environment, perform tasks, and carry out some analysis. They would realize when situations were beyond their abilities and request human help. And they would shut themselves down without damage. This could become necessary if, for instance, the weather or other conditions, such as toxic materials in the air or extreme heat or cold, became more extreme than the robots were designed to handle.

Vision and touch are the most important sensory systems needed in space robots. (From what scientists know about the Mars surface, there isn't anything to hear, smell, or taste.) For a scientist controlling a telerobot on the surface, the best sensory information would be provided by telepresence.

According to one NASA-sponsored study, telepresence requires a stereo color camera controlled by the scientist's head movements, allowing him or her to gaze at the distant landscape, look from side to side, focus on specific objects, and carefully observe the terrain the robot is standing on. This may require several lenses for each eye. And of course the computer program must merge the images into a stereo picture, as the human brain does for our own vision system.

Telepresence will also be valuable when humans land on the planet. Bundled in their spacesuits, they won't be able to directly feel the wind on their faces or touch the rocks with their fingertips. But telepresence, from robotic sensors on their suits, will give them the same experience.

The next step in telepresence could come from what is called "sensory substitution." This is when the brain substitutes one sense for another to provide information. It is well-known that people who have vision impairments can use their sense of touch to gain much "visual" information. Braille works on this principle.

Scientists have found that visual information can also be translated into touch information. This would allow cameras on Mars to transmit "touch" pictures through telepresence systems. This could work for telerobots and their operators and also for astronauts on the surface. Sound information can also be translated into touch information. This is now used for people with hearing impairments. Scientists also see an environmental sensing role for groups of the simple behavioral robots.

How will the robots get around on the Martian terrain? Some will roll on tires, using a system called CARD—Computer-Aided Remote Driving. CARD includes path planning by a remote operator making use of a 3-D vision system and robot-controlled navigation by dead reckoning. Others will walk on legs.

Robot Tasks on Mars

Analysis of the Martian surface is vital. The first robots on the planet will be able to identify minerals, pick up samples, and walk or roll across the landscape. In time robots should be able to prepare sites, assemble and build equipment, set up and maintain equipment, and make repairs. More intelligent robots will interpret data and even decide which samples are most useful in understanding the planet better.

Robots are expected to play important roles in the first phase of Mars exploration, called *Mesur* (the Mars Environmental SURvey mission), now under serious study by NASA. Mesur would set up a network of monitoring stations all over the planet. Over a two-year period, they would collect information about weather, earthquake patterns, and the structure and composition of the surface and the first meter (3 feet) below the surface. Robots would set up the seismometers that sense earthquakes. They would not only take soil samples but also perform tests such as X-ray spectrometry, to learn the samples' composition. (X-ray spectrometry identifies a material by the pattern of X rays bounced off of its various atoms.)

Space Robots Beyond the Mars Mission

The Mars robot explorers are expected to be followed by many more ambitious missions. Some of them could be launched from a space station. Round-trip missions will bring samples of Mars rock and soil back with them, perhaps early in the 21st century. According to a NASA study, intelligent robots would be landed by a spacecraft. They would find the samples and bring them to a return space vehicle. The vehicle could bring the samples to the space station where people and other robots would analyze them. By the year 2019, humans could step onto Mars, complete with robotic assistants. Beyond that? Scientists have seriously proposed turning all or part of Mars into an Earthlike habitat, complete with air that humans and other Earth life could breathe.

There is also interest in Venus. Our other neighbor planet has already had spacecraft landings by Soviet ships, in 1978–81. At some point in the future, robots or robot-human crews may land on that planet as well.

7 ROBOTS, SOCIETY —AND YOU

Robots will be part of our future, sometimes in unexpected places. They will be making things and selling them to us. They will be our coworkers. How will robotics affect our jobs? What will they mean to the whole U.S. economy? And a final question: Is there any limit to what robots can do?

One important issue is human safety around robots.

Working Safely with Robots

Working well with a partner requires cooperation. Each person must know what the other person is doing. They must keep out of each other's way. Even when people are "thinking safety," accidents can happen. Lifting and carrying a large, heavy object, for example, requires care that one of the carriers isn't bumped from behind by the object or pressed between the object and a wall.

When the partner is a robot, safety is very important. Robots can be heavy and speedy. Instead of a mild bump, a robot can deliver a blow leading to serious injury or even death.

Why do human-robot accidents happen? Sometimes an accident is the robot's fault. It may have moved unexpectedly, the same way a car lurches forward sometimes. Or the robot may drop a tool that hits someone. The robot can make the wrong move because of a computer error or a power failure. Or the robot might be turned on at the wrong time.

People sometimes get careless. They forget that robots are machines. Some of the accidents are the human workmate's fault, like entering the robot's workspace. For instance, if a person sees something jammed in a robot's hand, the instinct is to reach over and pull it out. As a result, the robot's hand grasps the human one. Or someone might enter the workspace by mistake, or for no particular reason. In some cases, workers have been hit from behind and pinned between the robot and another machine or a wall. If the robot is still, the worker may not even realize that it's turned on. More than one out of every three accidents is caused by the worker. That means that workers need safety training.

But the design of the robot and its workspace is also important. Experts recommend operating speed limits. Sensors can be installed to detect humans or objects that shouldn't be in the area. The robot's workspace should be fenced in. And there should be switches that stop the robot if someone or something enters its space. Of course, a robot that's designed to operate accurately and reliably is a safety plus.

Designing a robot to be accurate and reliable requires professional skill. Many robotics experts think social responsibility also plays a part; this is discussed below.

The "Three Laws of Robotics" Revisited

Isaac Asimov's Three Laws of Robotics say that robots can protect themselves as long as they don't disobey or harm people. Of course, robots are designed and built by people. So it's up to people to make sure that the Three Laws are designed into robots.

People must also decide how robots will be used. Computer science is already deeply involved in this problem. People have used computers to snoop into other people's private files. Some do this out of curiosity. Others enter files to steal money or information, or to destroy or change the information. Such actions are illegal. Each computer designer, manufacturer, and user must make choices. Each person must ask: How do I use the equipment to get what I need, without harming someone else or society as a whole? This is called *ethics*.

As robotics grows, the same questions will be asked about it—and some new questions, too. When robots can be sent on tasks far from the human operator, who is in control? What will we program them to do? As one scientist has asked, will we just end up as people armed with robots instead of guns?

Will Robots Replace People in the Workplace?

The increasing use of robots in the workplace has both good and bad points. Robots can do the same job over and over without making mistakes. They work 24 hours a day. There are many places where robots should replace people, for instance, working in radioactive environments. But according to government figures, even the fast food industry can be a dangerous place to work.

Every time jobs are taken over by robots, people are put out of work. Robots have already replaced some factory and service workers. This trend will continue. The reason is money. Robots can be expensive to buy, but they don't get sick, quit their jobs, need vacations, or want health insurance. For repetitive tasks and automated factories, robots can be an economical choice.

Also, some business executives think that today's workers have fewer skills than workers in the past did. The executives say this forces them to use automation and robots.

What happens to the people who are replaced? In the 1920s, the authors of *Metropolis* and *R.U.R.* worried about robots putting people out of work. Today the worries are still with us.

Sometimes the robots are used in the same factory where only people formerly worked. In these cases replacement is gradual and workers have an opportunity to seek different jobs. In other cases, entirely new factories are built, perhaps in other parts of town, in another state, or in another country. If the displaced workers live in big cities, they may find other jobs in the same industry, but this isn't always possible.

Of course, people can be retrained for different kinds of work. But society must decide who pays for their retraining and education. In addition, if other companies in the area don't need workers, must people move from their neighborhoods, hometowns, and regions to find work?

It has always been hard to turn away from automation. In the 1740s the king of France put Vaucanson, who built the Flute Player and the Duck, in charge of making the silk industry in Lyon more efficient. Vaucanson tried to turn the silk weavers' craft into a factory system. But the weavers didn't want to be factory workers. In 1746 they rioted. They even made up nasty songs about Vaucanson and his automated Duck. But 60 years later, Jacquard invented his loom in Lyon. His invention made modern weaving factories possible, as well as being a giant step toward computers and robots.

In the 1960s, American labor unions opposed using robots in factories because they didn't want their members to lose jobs. Now unions take part as factories automate. They help retrain the workers for other jobs, including installing robots.

Robotics and U.S. Industry

Robots could be very important in the United States in the next 10 years. But will they be?

The modern robotics industry began in the United States in the 1960s. But the United States has been slower to use industrial robots than other countries. Japan, Sweden, Germany, and Italy all use more. The United States has fewer than 40,000 industrial robots, while Japan, for instance, has over twice as many. Also, use is growing faster in these other countries.

Should U.S. industry use more robots? Many experts think it should, especially when robots are part of a flexible manufacturing system. They believe this could increase productivity and competitiveness.

We have a global economy. U.S. companies want to sell their products in many countries, not just at home. The best-selling products are well-made and cost less than the competition. When more U.S.-made products are sold around the world, more money will come back to the United States.

Automated factories can make the difference in quality and price. According to some economic studies, when a company automates its factories, it can design and build at least twice as many products as before. In other words, its productivity doubles. The cost is much lower, and quality may also improve. If U.S. industrial productivity doubled, it could bring $1 trillion ($1,000,000,000,000) more into the U.S. economy.

The future is sure to include robots, in factories and elsewhere in society. They probably will be more brainlike in operation and perhaps more able to perform intelligently. They may be different in other ways, too. Already scientific research is changing the relationship between people and robots.

Living Robots?

Living species—as defined by biologists—mate or otherwise reproduce, pass on their characteristics to their children, and evolve. Suppose there are other beings that do the same things but that are electronic, rather than chemical, as we are. They exist only in a computer's circuits. Are they alive, the way people, dogs, bacteria, or even viruses are? Are they *artificial life*?

Until recently, the idea of living robots was just that—an idea. Despite their inventors' efforts, 18th-century automatons were not alive. Since 1950, the computer has made people ask whether machines can think, and some people have answered Yes. Now, in the 1990s, can people also answer Yes to the question "can machines be alive?"

Artificial life is a type of computer program that behaves like a living organism, mating (interacting with other programs), reproducing (creating new programs), passing on characteristics according to the rules of genetics, competing with other programs, and evolving into very different programs.

Some artificial life programs use computer graphics to draw pictures of the "creatures." Each new generation appears on the screen, showing new characteristics and mutations. Some of them even develop into different species. They become predators and prey. Some species become dominant; others die out.

Some scientists say these "organisms" are very close to being alive. They fit the biological definition of life. These scientists think (or hope) the programs are erasing the line between living organisms and non-living matter. If so—and it is a big "if"—the same reasoning could be applied to advanced robots.

The main difference, of course, is that the artificial organisms "live" only within the computer—they are electronic. Robots, on the other hand, are made of matter and function in the real world. According to some computer scientists, the definition of "real world" is also changing. They believe that *cyberspace*, or *artificial reality*, is as real as the physical world. If the electronic world is "real," then robot controller brains could contain the computer programs of artificial life.

There are many ways you can take part in the world of robotics. One way is by knowing their place in industry and society as a whole. Some people prefer to become more involved, including hands-on experience.

Robots up Close

A good place to start looking for robots is a science museum near you. Many museums have exhibits that let people become the controller of a robotic arm. To find a museum, check the Yellow Pages, or ask a librarian or science teacher.

A high school shop teacher or computer science teacher may know if any local industries employ robots. Some companies are happy to arrange tours for student groups.

Another place to look is the computer science department of a university. Call the public affairs office (sometimes called press relations or media relations office) and ask.

The most thorough way to experience robots is to build one. In Japan, university students build robots each year to compete in sumo wrestling (traditional Japanese-style wrestling). Like human sumo wrestlers, the robots try to push each other out of the ring or knock each other over. One difference is that human sumo athletes often weigh over 300 pounds. Each sumo robot is less than a foot tall and weighs less than 10 pounds. A few U.S. universities also hold competitions, such as one at the University of California, Riverside. The winners of some of these U.S. competitions go to the contest in Japan.

There are two ways to build a robot. One can purchase a robot kit and put it together. One can also design, assemble, and program one's own.

[Courtesy of Michael Capriotti, University of California, Riverside]

A match between sumo-wrestling robots at the University of California, Riverside

Building a Robot

Robot Kits

A kit contains all the parts required for a working robot, along with instructions for assembling it. Besides the pleasure of quickly having the robot ready to operate, assembling a kit helps a newcomer understand the basics of electronic circuitry and the robot's working parts.

Most of the robots are small and battery operated. Many are mobile, with wheels or legs, and some have an arm and hand.

The simplest ones perform basic movements: start, stop, and go backward and forward. They are controlled from a hand-held switch box or control box attached to the robot by cable—teleoperation. Pushing a switch or pressing a button or a combination of buttons sends command signals for the robot to obey.

More complex robots have sensors, allowing them to react to their environment. Sound sensors register voices or hand claps. Other sound sensors detect ultrasonics, noises too high for human ears to

(Courtesy of MOVIT Division, OWI Incorporated)

This six-legged robot, called Spider, uses infrared sensing to change direction and walk around obstacles.

pick up. One robot even comes with a "silent" whistle. When someone blows the whistle, the robot's ultrasound sensor can detect the "sounds." This uses the same principle as the "silent" whistles used to train or control dogs, who can hear sounds people can't.

Infrared sensors let some robots follow dark lines on a light surface. This is the same principle used by some robotic service carts that deliver mail in buildings. Touch sensors stop a robot's motion when it bumps into something or allow the robot to detect obstacles and detour around them.

The most "advanced" kit robots can be programmed. Some use a keypad (like a handheld calculator keyboard) for entering commands. Some come with software and can be attached to computers—IBM-compatible PCs, Apple II, or Commodore. In some cases, the user can also write command software.

Robots from Scratch

What do you need to design and build a robot? This book has shown you what robots can do. Each robot at work in a factory or being tested in a research laboratory was developed from simpler experiments. Most people begin their first robot by deciding what they want it to do. After defining the task, the builder should make a list of the parts needed.

For instance, a mobile robot will require wheels or tracks. For a walking robot, the builder must decide which design and method of moving the legs to use. If the robot will grasp, lift, or carry something, it must have an arm and hand (manipulator and end effector).

The builder must also decide what the robot's world will be; where it will operate; what, if anything, it must know about its environment. If it should avoid objects, the builder will need a touch sensor and perhaps an infrared (heat) sensor.

A knowledge of electronics is important. Many robot builders read magazines such as *Popular Electronics* or *Radio Electronics*. Large bookstores and some electronics stores carry books on the basics of electronics. A computer science teacher may also provide information or help.

The builder also needs a way to control the robot. If the design requires only a few commands, a switch box or control box is appropriate. Joysticks—like those on some video games, electronic toys, or computers—can also be used. For a larger number of commands, a keypad and two- or three-digit command codes will probably be necessary.

Putting the control commands in a computer program gives you the most flexibility. This, of course, requires connecting the robot to a computer. The simplest way is to use the computer's parallel printer port. This will require a relay, which converts computer logic signals to switch-contact signals. The computer manual or other reference defines the pin signals for parallel communications, so the builder can design the wiring correctly.

The program will contain all the commands. Many people write robot programs in BASIC. Another language is Logo, which is an adaptation of the AI language Lisp. Logo was designed to draw graphics with a robotlike device. The language recognizes commands like MOVE, TURN, and FORWARD, and in this way is similar to languages for commercial robots.

Robot scientists are serious and well-educated professionals. They do serious work. But most of them have another characteristic. They love robots and think building and working with them is fun!

People who want to take part in the world of robotics can learn many things about robots. The experience can also allow the builder the opportunity to learn more about him- or herself and to have fun doing it.

GLOSSSARY

Action A useful motion that a robot makes, like lifting, assembling, or moving something.

Actuator The system that makes a robot's arm move, like a motor or an air-powered or fluid-powered system.

AI See *artficial intelligence*

Android Robot that looks and acts human and thinks intelligently. No androids exist.

Anthropomorphic Like a human; describing a non-human in human terms. For example, using *arm* to describe a robot's manipulator.

Artificial intelligence (AI) A computer or robot's ability to think or do work that is just like human thought or action.

Artificial neural network See *neural network*

Associative memory The human brain's method of storing information by its content and meaning, so that a small clue can bring whole images or ideas to mind.

Automation Self-operating machine in the days before computers; operated by mechanical energy or water power.

Autonomous Characteristic of a robot that moves and works entirely on its own.

Axon In the human nervous system, a fiber that brings incoming signals to a nerve cell (neuron).

Backward chaining In artificial intelligence, forming a possible answer to a problem, then working backward through a series (chain) of rules to see if they support it.

Certainty factors Numbers used in some expert systems to give different grades of importance to different uncertain facts and information.

Chance How likely something is to happen, like "there is a 50 percent chance of rain today."

Charge-coupled device (CCD) A camera that uses a computer chip instead of film. Used in some robotic vision systems.

"Chinese room" An AI problem in which a person who can't read Chinese must process cards filled with Chinese characters according to a strict set of rules. Is the person doing intelligent work?

Computer integrated manufacturing (CIM) See *flexible manufacturing system*

Continuous path control Robotic motion in which only the beginning and ending points are set. The controller calculates stopping points in between.

Controller A computer that is in charge of a robot's overall operations.

Cortex Brain area where information is processed and stored and where thought takes place.

Cybernetics The science of systems, especially the way the body's systems work like mechanical systems that do the same things. An example is the vision system.

Cyborg A being that is part human and part robot. No cyborgs exist.

Dead reckoning Method of navigation relying solely on the speed and direction of movement.

Decision maker Computer program that decides whether a robot should perform an operation.

Dedicated Descriptive of a computer that performs just one operation, such as taking in information from a robotic sensor.

Deep reasoning Reasoning that analyzes knowledge, experience, or a problem to find out its basic structure.

Degree of freedom (DOF) Measure of a manipulator's flexibility. Each joint means one degree of freedom.

Dendrite A nervous system fiber that carries outgoing signals from a nerve cell (neuron).

Dexterous or dextrous Very flexible, like the human hand. In a robot, an arm or hand with many degrees of freedom.

DOF See *degree of freedom*

Domain Term used in artificial intelligence to describe an expert's specialty, such as medical diagnosis or oil-drilling.

End effector A robot's hand—the part that performs a task or holds a tool to perform a task.

Expert system AI computer program containing an expert's knowledge and method of problem-solving. Also called a knowledge-based system.

First generation expert system An expert system that uses shallow reasoning.

Fixed stop Type of robot whose moving manipulator can stop only at pre-set points.

Flexible manufacturing system or **computer integrated manufacturing (CIM)** Automated factory system in which computers control most operations, including the use of robots.

Forward chaining In artificial intelligence, working through a series (chain) of rules to reach a conclusion or solve a problem.

Fully autonomous See *autonomous*

Generalization An intelligent ability to take a specific situation and apply its characteristics to other situations.

Graphics-based programming Method of teaching a robot by designing its motions in a computer graphics program, then transferring them to the actual robot.

Gripper a robotic end effector, such as tongs, suction cup, or magnet, that grasps and holds an object.

Heuristic reasoning See *shallow reasoning*

Hierarchy A group's arrangement of operation by several levels. One level may be more important or complex than another. Or one level may control another level.

Hippocampus Brain area that coordinates memories stored in various parts of the cortex.

Hydraulic Characteristic of the use of pressurized oil or other fluid for robotic motion.

Hypothesis A possible solution to a problem

Image analysis Finding the meaning in an image seen by the human eye or a robot's vision system.

Intelligent teleoperated Descriptive of a robot, operated by a human, that has some computer control of the manipulator. Such a robot is called a telerobot.

Interface The part of a computer program that a person sees and uses.

Introspection An intelligent robot's ability to examine its own reasoning methods.

Joint Flexible connecting point on a robot, like the "elbow" where two arm links meet or the "wrist" where an arm and hand meet.

Knowledge-based system See *expert system*

Lead-through programming Method of teaching a robot by moving its arm through the motions. Each starting and stopping point is recorded for playback on the job.

Link A rigid part of a robot's manipulator (arm), similar to a human bone.

Lisp A computer language, used in artificial intelligence, that processes lists of items.

Machine tools Machines that can perform simple factory operations without human help, but are not as flexible and intelligent as robots.

Manipulator A robot's arm, which moves and performs a task.

Master-slave manipulator Simple robotic arm that is controlled by a human operator's (master's) hand movements on one end. The arm and hand (slave) perform the same movements at the other end.

Memory A person's knowledge and experiences, stored in the brain.

Microrobot A robot too small for a human to see with the naked eye, for instance, one that is 100 micrometers (μm) in diameter.

Mind The thought processes of the human brain.

Natural language processing Computer analysis of human language so it can be used in artificial intelligence.

Neural network Computer or computer program that solves problems in a brainlike way. It finds the best path that leads from a question to its answer, such as by recognizing patterns.

Neuron A brain cell or a nerve cell.

Node A place where two lines or paths meet. In a neural network, a place where information is transferred from one path to another.

Nonmonotonic reasoning Reasoning in uncertain conditions.

Numerical control Method of programming a machine tool that uses numbers to describe the tool and its movements.

Optical computer Computer that uses lasers or other light to process information, instead of using electronic circuits.

Pantograph A series of adjustable parallelogram-shaped armatures used as a leg or arm system in some robots.

Parallel distributed processing The way the brain processes information. It processes many parts of a problem at the same time and in many different brain locations.

Parallel processing Use of several computer chips to work on different parts of a problem at the same time.

Pick-and-place A type of robot that picks up an item and sets it down in another place.

Planner An intelligent computer program that sets goals and priorities for problem-solving.

Playback See *record and playback robot*

Pneumatics Use of pressurized air for robotic motion.

Point-to-point control Robotic motion system in which the robot can stop only at points it has already been taught to stop at.

Probability The chance that something may happen, or the degree to which something will happen. For instance, a 50 percent chance that it will rain today.

Processor A computer.

Program A list of computer instructions that tells a robot how to perform a task.

Prolog Computer language used in artificial intelligence to write rules for problem solving. It can handle uncertainty.

Real time Time as measured by a clock or one's body. Robots must be able to perform tasks or solve problems in real time.

Record and playback robot A robot whose motions are taught and recorded with lead-through programming, then played back on the job.

Remotely operated vehicle (ROV) Type of underwater vehicle that is controlled remotely by communication lines (usually tethers) from ships or platforms. Some ROVs are robotic, with arms and specialized hands.

Second generation expert system Type of expert system that uses deep reasoning.

Semantics The meaning of language.

Sensor A human organ that measures touch, sound, light, odor, or taste. A robot part that measures such factors of the robot's environment as light, sound, touch, or temperature.

Sequential processing See *serial processing*

Serial processing or **sequential processing** Computer processing of one item at a time. The method used by most computers.

Servo-controlled Descriptive of a robot controlled by a *servomechanism.*

Servomechanism A device that knows where a robot's joint or arm is in relation to its possible range and feeds the information back to the controller.

Shallow reasoning or **heuristic reasoning** Reasoning that takes past experience and makes easy-to-use rules out of it.

Somatosensory cortex Portion of the human brain that finds the meaning of information from the hand's touch sensors.

Strain gauge Instrument used as a robotic force and torque sensor.

Submersible Small submarine that carries a crew and sometimes passengers. Some submersibles are robotic, with arms and specialized hands. The research vessel *Alvin* is an example.

Supervised autonomy Robotic control using computer decision-making, but allowing a human to take back control.

Synapse Place in the nervous system where the outgoing signal from one nerve cell (neuron) becomes the incoming signal of another nerve cell.

Syntax The structure of language.

Teach pendant A control box that records the starting and stopping points taught to a robot with lead-through programming.

Teleoperated Characteristic of a robot that is operated by a human, much like a master-slave manipulator.

Telepresence Remote sensing of the environment that gives a human operator the sensation of being in direct contact. A feature of intelligent robotics.

Telerobot An intelligent teleoperated robot.

Tether An electronic line between a human operator and a telerobot that transmits commands, information, and sometimes the robot's electric power.

Torque Twisting.

Track A motion system in which wheels roll inside an endless belt or tread. Used in some mobile robots, it is same method used on earth-moving machines.

Translation A robotic movement in which two parts stay in the same relative directions. For example, two parts of a sliding joint, which move like a sliding door.

Turing test The test to show whether a computer can think, devised by Alan Turing. The computer must perform an intelligent act so that a human expert can't tell whether it was done by a human or a computer.

Uncertainty That quality displayed by a situation or question that cannot be understood or answered with Yes or No.

Visual cortex Portion of the human brain that processes images that the eyes see.

Work path The straight or curved path a robotic arm follows as it performs a task.

World The part of the total environment that an individual or a robot can measure with senses or sensors and interpret or understand.

FURTHER READING

Asimov, Isaac, and Frenkel, Karen A. *Robots: Where the Machine Ends and Life Begins*. New York: Harmony House, 1985. An overview of robotics by Isaac Asimov, the late popularizer of science fact, who was also a science fiction writer and the author of the Three Laws of Robotics. The book is now somewhat out-of-date.

Capek, Karel. *R.U.R. (Rossum's Universal Robots)*, translated by Paul Selver. New York: Doubleday, Page & Co., 1923. The play that introduced the word *robot*. This edition is interesting because it contains photographs of the first New York performance of the play. This and other editions of the book are available in major public libraries. Library systems that do not hold the book can usually obtain a copy through interlibrary loan.

Electric Power Research Institute. *A Compendium of Robotic Equipment Used in Hazardous Environments*. Electric Power Research Institute Report EPRI NP-6697, February 1990. Available from EPRI, 3412 Hillview Ave., Palo Alto, California 94304. A compilation of all known robots designed for or used in hazardous environments, including the specifications for each robot and a photograph if available.

Heiserman, David. *How to Design and Build Your Own Custom Robot*. Blue Ridge Summit, Pennsylvania: TAB Books, 1981. A practical guide to building a robot from scratch. The book shows projects that could be challenging for beginners.

Krasnoff, Barbara. *Robots: Reel to Real*. New York: Arco Publishing, 1982. An entertaining, though somewhat out-of-date, overview of robots as depicted in the movies.

Papert, Seymour *Mindstorms: Children, Computers, and Powerful Ideas*. New York: Basic Books, Inc., 1980. Description of the computer language Logo by its major author, along with the philosophy behind it. The book contains a good explanation of Logo and how it can be used for education and entertainment.

However, some sections of the book may be too theoretical for some young people.

Poe, Edgar Allan. *The Complete Edgar Allan Poe Tales.* New York: Crown Publishers, 1981. "The Man That Was Used Up," on p. 192, is the first American work of fiction to depict a forerunner of a cyborg; by the "father of the detective story."

Thro, Ellen. *The Artificial Intelligence Dictionary.* San Marcos, California: Microtrend Books, Slawson Communications, 1991. A plain-language dictionary covering the major concepts of robotics and artificial intelligence.

Ride, Dr. Sally K. "Leadership and America's Future in Space, A Report to the Administrator," U.S. National Aeronautics and Space Administration, August 1987. A plan for the future missions of NASA, including missions to the moon and Mars in which robots would play a prominent part. Budget restrictions and priority changes may eventually change the character of the missions described in what some call "the Ride report."

INDEX

Italic numbers indicate illustrations.